A2 Sociology
UNIT 5

AQA

Module 5: Theory and Methods

Emma Jones, Marsha Jones & Joan Garrod

Series Editor: Joan Garrod

For Lola, Lillian and Peter

Philip Allan Updates
Market Place
Deddington
Oxfordshire
OX15 0SE

Tel: 01869 338652
Fax: 01869 337590
e-mail: sales@philipallan.co.uk
www.philipallan.co.uk

This Guide has been written specifically to support students preparing for the AQA A2 Sociology Unit 5 examination. The content has been neither approved nor endorsed by AQA and remains the sole responsibility of the authors.

Printed by Raithby, Lawrence & Co. Ltd, Leicester

A2 Sociology

Contents

Introduction

■ ■ ■

Content Guidance

■ ■ ■

Questions and Answers

■ ■ ■

A2 Coursework Task

Introduction

About this guide

This unit guide is for students in their second year (A2) of sociology A-level. It deals with a very important area in sociology: **Theory and Methods**. Although you will already have studied research methods in your AS year, this topic is more detailed and deals with theoretical issues and debates about the nature of science and whether we can categorise sociology as a scientific discipline. This guide provides you with an overview of these issues, but you will need to be familiar with the detailed aspects of the topic from your lessons and textbooks. There are four sections to this guide:

- **Introduction** — this provides guidance on how to make the best use of the guide; it offers help with revision and provides an outline of the assessment aims of A2. It also gives advice on how to be successful in the unit test. Some students will be choosing to submit a piece of coursework rather than sitting the unit test. Coursework guidance appears in the fourth section of the guide.
- **Content Guidance** — this provides details of the specification subsections of Theory and Methods. (Be sure not to leave anything out of your revision as the unit test may question any aspect of theory and methodology.) Each topic area of the guide lists the main ideas of that theory/method, its strengths and limitations, key concepts and key thinkers.
- **Questions and Answers** — this provides some examples of questions from Theory and Methods that you might be faced with in the unit test. Each question has examples of students' responses to show how the question can be addressed. There are also examiner's comments to show how marks are allocated. The final question is for you to try yourself.
- **A2 Coursework Task** — this gives guidance to candidates submitting a piece of coursework rather than sitting the unit test.

How to use the guide

To use this guide to your best advantage, you should refer to the Introduction and Content Guidance sections from the beginning of your study of Theory and Methods. However, we would recommend that you do not attempt the questions in the Question and Answer section until you feel confident with the topic. Then take each in turn, study it carefully and answer the different parts. Try to avoid reading the candidates' responses until you have completed your own. In this way you will get a better idea of where your answer lies in relation to the given responses. When you have done this, study the grade-A candidate's answer carefully, as this should demonstrate what the examiners are looking for. You might also try to improve on the grade-C candidate's response using the examiner's comments.

Don't be disheartened if you find the questions a little daunting. Theories in sociology are by no means simple to understand and you need to be able to make connections between theories and methodology. So read the relevant sections of your textbooks and look carefully at the Content Guidance section of this book before tackling the questions.

The A2 specification

The aims of the A2 sociology course are to enable you to:
- acquire knowledge and a critical understanding of contemporary social processes and structures
- appreciate the significance of theoretical and conceptual issues in sociological debate
- understand sociological methodology and a range of research methods
- reflect on your own experience of the social world in which you live
- develop skills that enhance your ability to participate more effectively in adult life

At A2 you will also be expected to have acquired a *deeper* understanding of the connections between the nature of sociological thought, methods of sociological enquiry and substantive sociological topics.

Examinable skills

A2 sociology examinations are designed to test certain skills. These skills, or 'Assessment Objectives', are common to both AS and A2, but their weighting differs. There are two main Assessment Objectives. At A2, AO1 is worth 40% and AO2 is worth 60% of the total marks.

Assessment Objective 1

Assessment Objective 1 (AO1) is 'knowledge and understanding'. These skills are clearly linked and you must show the examiner not only that you have the necessary knowledge, but that you are able to use it in a meaningful way. Understanding implies that you can select the relevant knowledge and use it appropriately in response to a question. AO1 covers:
- the nature of sociological thought
- methods of sociological enquiry
- themes

The nature of sociological thought
This includes the following:
- social order, social control and social changes
- conflict and consensus

- social structure and social action
- macro and micro perspectives
- the nature of social facts
- the role of values
- the relationship between sociology and social policy

Methods of sociological enquiry

You are required to be familiar with the range of methods and sources of data involved in sociological research. You also need to understand the relationship between theory and methods, especially the way sociologists deal with:

- the acquisition of primary and secondary data through observation, interviews and documents
- the analysis of quantitative and qualitative data using appropriate concepts
- factors influencing the design and execution of sociological research
- ethical issues arising in sociological research

Themes

You are required to study two themes that run throughout the course. You will be expected to know how they relate to topics within sociology. They are:

- socialisation, culture and identity
- social differentiation, power and stratification

Assessment Objective 2

Assessment Objective 2 (AO2) covers identification, analysis, interpretation and evaluation. You will be expected to demonstrate your ability to:

- **identify** facts, opinion and value judgements
- **analyse and evaluate** the design of a range of investigations
- **analyse and evaluate** the methods used to collect, select and record relevant evidence
- **interpret** research findings and secondary data to **identify** social trends
- **evaluate** different theories, arguments and evidence

In addition, you will be expected to present your arguments coherently, to show your awareness of theoretical debates in sociology and to use evidence to support and sustain your arguments and conclusions.

Study skills and revision strategies

- As well as reading and making notes, you should try to read a quality newspaper such as the *Guardian*, the *Independent* or the *Observer* at least once a week. The *Guardian* has sections dedicated to media, education and society that are of particular sociological interest. This will provide you with contemporary examples that you can refer to in your essays.

- Surf the net! There are now some excellent websites dedicated to AS and A2 sociology.
- If you do not already subscribe to *Sociology Review* yourself, your school or college library probably does. Read back copies. This journal is invaluable for keeping you up-to-date with sociological research and for providing good advice for exams.
- For each of your A-level units, make sure that you know what the awarding board specifies as necessary knowledge. Make notes on each of these areas and keep them in a revision folder separate from your class notes.
- Above all, be organised — make yourself an examination timetable at least 2 months before the exams start and fill in the dates and times when you will be revising each topic area.
- When you finally reach the week(s) of the exams themselves, get a good night's sleep each night. Do *not* stay up until the early hours trying to get in some last-minute revision — you might fall asleep in the exam!
- In the exam, allocate your time carefully, making sure that you allow enough time to write the essay as well as answering the shorter questions.

The unit test

Theory and Methods is the Module 5 topic in the A2 course. Candidates who choose not to attempt the coursework module will have to sit this unit test instead. The test is 1½ hours long and is equivalent to 15% of the total A-level marks. Although as part of your AS course you will have studied sociological research methods and may even have sat the Unit 3 test, this module demands more depth of understanding and more awareness of the sociological theories of society as well as the debates surrounding sociology as a scientific discipline.

The unit test is divided into Section A — a data–response section marked out of 20 — and Section B — an essay section marked out of 40, where you will have a choice of one essay from two.

In **Section A** there are two **items** to respond to, as there were for the AS modules (note, however, that Units 4 and 6 will have only one item). This section will usually have four questions marked out of 2, 4, 6 and 8 respectively, as was the case with AS questions. These shorter questions are likely to address aspects of the two items.

The essay questions in **Section B** will not necessarily relate directly to the items in Section A. As well as addressing issues that arise from the choice and use of research methods, the essays will also address questions relating to sociological theory.

The assessment objectives at A2 are different from those in the AS unit tests. The data–response section is weighted towards AO2, which takes 15 out of the 20 available marks. However, each essay is equally balanced 20/20 between AO1 and AO2.

Content Guidance

This section is intended as a guide through the **Theory and Methods** specification. It aims to show you the strengths and limitations of the various methods used by sociologists together with brief examples of studies that have used these methods. It also outlines the key concepts, thinkers and basic assumptions of the sociological theories that you have encountered throughout your course. As we have maintained with the earlier *Student Unit Guides* in the series, the guidance here is neither exhaustive nor exclusive. You will be familiar with the material from your work in class and from your study of the recommended textbooks. Don't forget that back copies of *Sociology Review* will be an invaluable source of up-to-date articles on research and debates in sociology.

It is essential that you are able to draw links with other topic areas you have studied and with the synoptic topics of **Crime and Deviance** and/or **Stratification and Differentiation**. After all, sociology is studied through the application of theory and the use of particular methodologies.

The Content Guidance section of this book is a brief outline of the relevant theories and the sociological methods for examination in Unit 5: Theory and Methods. Those of you who opt to undertake the coursework element will not be entered for this examination. However, you will be expected to be familiar with the material in this unit, as it links with all the substantive topics on the A-level course.

Module content

The A2 topic of Theory and Methods is designed to give you an in-depth understanding of sociological theory and methods, and how they are interlinked. It is, therefore, essential that you are able to:

- **adopt a more critical, evaluative and interpretative approach to the range of methodological issues than at AS**
- **study the nature of sociological enquiry in greater range and depth, and demonstrate more highly developed critical appraisal, evaluative and reflective skills, than at AS**

The content of Theory and Methods follows this pattern:

- the different quantitative and qualitative methods and sources of data, including questionnaires, interviews, observation techniques and experiments, and documents and official statistics
- the distinctions between primary and secondary data and between quantitative and qualitative data
- the relationship between positivism, interpretivism and sociological methods
- the theoretical, practical and ethical considerations influencing the choice of topic, the choice of methods and the conduct of research
- the nature of social facts and the strengths and limitations of different sources of data and methods of research

In addition, candidates should examine:

- consensus, conflict and social action theories
- the concepts of modernity and postmodernity in relation to sociological theory
- the nature of 'science' and the extent to which sociology may be regarded as scientific
- the relationship between theory and methods
- debates about subjectivity and value-freedom
- the relationship between sociology and social policy

SOCIOLOGICAL THEORIES

Consensus and conflict

Functionalism

Key ideas

- Functionalism is a macro approach — society is seen as a social system consisting of system parts, functionally interdependent and interrelated.
- Functionalism uses the organic analogy — society is seen as a living organism or mechanism. Change in one part will have effects elsewhere and a 'diseased' part will contaminate others.
- For Parsons, society has a set of needs or functional imperatives that are met by the four subsystems: economic, political, kinship and cultural.
- Social order is maintained through value consensus, whereby values are internalised through the early socialisation process and individuals learn the social norms and values of their social position. Interdependence is created through the division of labour and the obligations of social relationships.
- Conflict is minimised as individuals accept the inevitability and necessity of social inequalities (individuals have different talents and abilities).
- Society is made up of system parts such as family, education, religion and media, which all reinforce social solidarity.

Evaluation

- + Functionalism was the first major attempt to produce a grand theory of society.
- + It demonstrates successfully that social institutions are linked together.
- + It allows us to understand the functions (manifest and latent) of social rituals and social institutions.
- + It examines the importance of primary socialisation for any social order to be possible.
- − It places too much emphasis on harmony and fails to take into account competing power interests.
- − It fails to provide an adequate explanation of social change. All change is seen as evolutionary — which may not be the case.
- − It is accused of accepting the status quo and thus taking an inherently conservative view of society.
- − It is sometimes seen as teleological, i.e. as trying to explain the origins of any social institution by the function it performs for society — for example, the function of religion is seen as reinforcing social solidarity.

Key concepts

social solidarity; function; social order; social integration; interdependency;

interrelatedness; harmony; consensus; system parts; social institutions; social roles; equilibrium; goal attainment; adaptation; integration; latency

Key thinkers
Durkheim, Parsons, Davis and Moore, Merton.

New Right (neo-functionalism)

The ideas of the New Right became popular in the 1980s. They were associated with the work of Charles Murray and adopted by the US President Ronald Reagan and the British Prime Minister Margaret Thatcher. New Right ideas have been applied in sociology to the family, education and social stratification.

Key ideas

- New Right thinking is based on nineteenth-century liberalism, in which the free market was seen as the key to a successful economy.
- It favours less state intervention because it is assumed that state benefits create a dependency culture which takes away individual motivation to work and achieve.
- Murray maintained that the underclass in the USA was the major cause of criminality and immorality.
- Individual choice in areas such as pensions, education and medicine should be encouraged and people should be helped to buy their own property.
- There was interest in the revival of 'traditional' values and beliefs, especially surrounding the family and the value of hard work. Some lone-parent families were seen as causing major social problems.
- New Right supporters argue that state institutions such as local government, social services, education and the health services would be more efficient if they were run within a market-led system.

Evaluation
+ New Right thinking focuses on the importance of the individual's responsibility to the rest of society.
+ It attempts to find the causes of social problems.
+ Public–private partnerships stem from New Right thinking.
– Although the New Right advocated a rolling back of the state, it actually supported the introduction of harsher measures of social control.
– New Right ideas are more a political perspective than a theory of society.

Key concepts
marketisation; underclass; efficiency; rationalisation; competition; dependency culture

Key thinkers
Murray, Marsland, Wilson.

Marxism

There are several forms of Marxism, which have various names: classical Marxism is sometimes referred to as instrumentalist Marxism; neo-Marxism is often called hegemonic Marxism; and the Frankfurt School has a separate set of characteristics. We can see, however, that all forms share several basic assumptions.

Key ideas

- Marxism is a macro approach where society is seen as a social system based on relationships arising out of conflicts of interest.
- Society is divided between the **infrastructure** (the economic base, made up of the social relations of production and the forces of production) and the **super-structure** (social institutions such as the family, religion, law, education, politics and the mass media, which serve to legitimise the power relations arising from the infrastructure).
- The main focus of Marxism rests on the historical development and social relations of western capitalism. In capitalist society, the owners of private property in the means of production, the **bourgeoisie**, exploit the labour power of the non-owners, the **proletariat**.
- Social change is inevitable until the eventual achievement of a communist society. Revolution is the outcome of the process by which the subject classes gain awareness of their exploited situation and rise against the bourgeoisie.
- Hegemonic Marxism emphasises the role of ideology in maintaining the rule of the powerful. They keep their position by winning the consent of the subject groups through ideological persuasion.

Evaluation

- + Marxism has been a major force in social thought, influencing the progress of actual social change.
- + It has influenced other critical social thinkers within sociology, such as Weber and feminists.
- + Like functionalism, Marxism attempts to link the individual to the structure of society. Unlike functionalism, it emphasises socialisation into a capitalist society for the benefit of the powerful groups.
- − Classical Marxism is sometimes seen as overly deterministic. The individual is seen mainly as a passive victim of historical circumstance. However, neo-Marxists allow for some relative autonomy in the elements within the superstructure.
- − Functionalists criticise the over-emphasis on conflict — they see strengths in the existence of a value consensus.
- − Classical Marxism ignored gender relations in society by privileging social class in its analysis.
- − Postmodernists have strongly challenged Marxism for its metanarrative — recent social changes in the Eastern Bloc and China have served to undermine Marxism.

exploitation; oppression; subjugation; ideology; conflict; legitimation; alienation

Marx, Engels, Gramsci, Althusser, Marcuse, Adorno, Horkheimer.

Feminism

There are several branches of feminism — liberal feminism, Marxist feminism/feminist Marxism, radical feminism, black feminism and postmodern feminism — but they all share some basic assumptions.

Key ideas

- Gender relations are based on power and economic inequalities.
- Gender roles are socially constructed.
- Gender inequalities are largely social, not based on biological difference.
- Previously sociology was 'malestream' and ignored the social position of women in its theories.
- **Liberal feminism** is concerned with gender inequalities within education, the family and the work sphere. It focuses upon equal opportunities and legislation for change.
- **Marxist feminism** and **feminist Marxism** examine gender inequalities as they arise within capitalism. They focus on dual labour theory and the domestic labour debate. Feminist Marxists are particularly interested in the role of ideology within capitalism.
- **Radical feminism** emphasises the impact of patriarchy and sexual politics on women and children. Domestic violence is seen as a manifestation of patriarchy, as is pornography and sex-trafficking. Some radical feminists take a lesbian separatist position and advocate separatism between men and women.
- **Black feminism** concentrates specifically on the oppression of black women, as other forms of feminism failed to address issues of gender and race.
- **Postmodern feminism** challenges the earlier assumptions around gender identity, as it sees individuals benefiting from a range of female and male identities. Gender and sexual identity are seen as fluid.

+ Feminism made the role of women and gender relations visible — both in sociology and in society in general.
+ Feminists have exposed the dark side of family life, helping to free women and children from domestic violence and abuse.
+ Feminists have increased people's awareness of the inequalities created by gender.
+ They have shown how gender roles are socially constructed.
+ Black feminists have exposed the colour-blindness of mainstream sociology.

- Feminists are accused of ignoring the domestic labour of men and the increasing economic and educational achievement of women.
- They ignore the element of choice in gender relationships.
- Marxist feminists fail to examine the oppression of women under state socialism.
- They produce a highly selective view of society.

Key concepts

gender; patriarchy; oppression; domestic labour

Key thinkers

Barret, Dworkin, Firestone, Millet, Oakley, Rowbotham, Walby.

Social action theory

Interpretivism

The interpretivist approach in sociology has several branches. We are mainly concerned with those known as Weberian sociology (verstehen sociology), symbolic interactionism and ethnomethodology. They share some basic assumptions, but also have specific characteristics.

Key ideas

- Social reality is constructed through the actions and interactions of individuals.
- Individuals define and interpret situations, negotiate meanings and thus create social reality.
- Sociologists must discover the meanings and interpretations of individuals in social action by placing themselves in the social positions of those individuals and gaining an empathetic understanding.
- **Symbolic interactionism** examines the use of 'symbols' such as language and gestures in social action. It uses the concept of **self** (the 'I' and the 'me') to show that individuals are self-reflexive and that, by using their understanding of past experiences, they can modify present action. Use of the dramaturgical metaphor (Goffman referred to social reality as a stage) allows us to see how social actors in social roles present their various 'selves' to the world. **Labelling theory** emerged from this approach. Labelling theorists emphasise the power of those who label and the effects on those who are labelled — once labelled as 'deviant', it is difficult to lose the label.
- In **verstehen sociology**, Weber uses ideal types of social action (rational, value-rational, traditional and affectual) to impose meaning on social reality. Only through empathetic interpretation of the meanings and motivations of individuals in social positions is sociology possible.

- **Ethnomethodology** examines the methods by which individuals make sense of everyday reality. Social reality is seen as precarious and, therefore, as constantly being accomplished by individuals. Social order depends on taken-for-granted assumptions or rules of everyday life; when these are challenged, anxiety is created. Language is indexical — it can change meaning according to the context.

Evaluation

+ These are micro approaches that see the individual as having agency, not simply as a recipient of external social forces.
+ Interpretivism enables us to see how social reality is constructed through meanings and negotiations.
- Verstehen sociology assumes that individuals engage in rational behaviour and thus are able to understand their own motivations. Ideal types are simply devices to make sense of chaotic reality. Weber's interpretation of the relationship between capitalism and Protestantism has been challenged on historical grounds.
- Symbolic interactionism ignores the impact of structural elements on individuals.
- Labelling assumes that social actors passively accept being labelled and tends to ignore resistance to labels.

Key concepts

interaction; negotiation; social construction; secondary deviance; the self; labelling; verstehen; indexicality; typifications

Key thinkers

Mead, Cooley, Weber, Becker, Schutz, Goffman, Garfinkel, Lemert.

Modernity and postmodernism

Modernity and postmodernity are concepts that define particular periods in social history and thought. There is an ongoing debate in sociology as to whether society has moved from modernity to postmodernity.

Modernity

Key ideas

- Enlightenment ideas in the eighteenth century influenced the social thinkers of the nineteenth century.
- Modernists held a strong belief in progress. In different ways Comte, Durkheim, Marx and Weber all saw western societies as moving towards a 'better world'.

The application of science, rationality and technology would inevitably produce social progress.
- Objective knowledge became both desirable and possible.
- Modernists believed that they could apply scientific methodology to the study of society in order to understand it and bring about desired social changes.
- Overall, modernity was an optimistic view of the future of society.

Postmodernism

Key ideas

- Postmodernists do not accept the ideas of the Enlightenment — they do not believe in the power of science to solve all social and environmental problems. In fact, science and technology can be blamed for destroying the environment. It is a pessimistic approach that sees the future of society as **dystopic**.
- They have challenged social theorists by maintaining that the metanarratives or 'big stories' of the past, such as Marxism and functionalism, are insufficient to make sense of our changing world. Knowledge is no longer absolute but dependent and relative.
- The development of the mass media and global communications through computers have encouraged us to define ourselves through cultural and media images. The old certainties of social class, gender and race have been fractured and fragmented, and an individual's identity is now more reliant on media imagery.
- Time and space have been compressed through communications and travel — cultures have become **hybridised**.

Evaluation

+ Postmodernism has tried to interpret the new social and cultural changes, such as the opening up of the Eastern Bloc.
+ It has attempted to analyse the growing impact of mass media on society.
+ It challenges the absolutist positions of the old metanarratives.
+ It sees individuals as having choices to create 'pick and mix' identities through consumerism.
- Postmodernism is a confusing theoretical approach, as different thinkers emphasise different aspects.
- In challenging the metanarratives, it is in danger of becoming a new theoretical position in itself.
- Postmodernism emphasises the cultural at the expense of the social and economic.
- It fails to recognise the constraints on individuals of the huge social inequalities that still exist based on economics, gender and ethnicity.
- It is seen as overplaying the role of the mass media and taking a relatively passive view of the individual as audience member.

metanarratives; simulacra; hyperreality; hybridisation; language games

Lyotard, Baudrillard, Harvey.

Science and sociology

The debate about whether sociology can be scientific depends on what definition of science is applied. There is some controversy as to how far natural science follows 'scientific' principles.

Science and the sociological perspectives

Positivism

- Natural science is based on the hypothetico-deductive method and searches for cause and effect relationships between phenomena. The scientist seeks to discover the underlying laws that govern nature.
- It is both possible and necessary for scientists to be objective and value-free.
- Scientific knowledge is both cumulative and falsifiable (Popper).

Interpretivism

- The scientific method is appropriate only to natural phenomena where there is no question of consciousness or reflexivity.
- The scientific method cannot be applied to the understanding of social action.

Kuhn

- As a challenge to Popper, Kuhn maintains that science is not a cumulative body of knowledge.
- Most scientists work within a given academic community using a shared paradigm (a complete theory and framework of methodology within which scientists operate).
- Scientific revolutions occur when the assumptions of normal science are challenged by anomalies that cannot be covered by the existing paradigm.

Kaplan

He distinguishes between **reconstructed logics** (methods and procedures that scientists claim to use) and **logics in use** (what actually takes place in scientific research). Phenomena might be dismissed as 'artefacts' if they do not fit the pre-existing theoretical assumptions.

Marxism

- Science is not value-free but responds to demands of capitalism — profit and ideology.
- Scientific research is dominated by competition, the profit motive and ideological justification of the interests of powerful groups.

Feminism

- Science is essentially a patriarchal institution.
- As the majority of scientists have been men, the scientific establishment emphasises malestream values.
- Scientists have attempted to justify the social inferiority of women by ideologically based research.
- Science prioritises aspects of society that are more beneficial to men, such as space exploration.

Realism

- Realists see science as an attempt to explain causal relationships in terms of underlying (unobservable) structures, mechanisms and processes.
- There are differences between **open** and **closed** systems in natural science.
- Within closed systems, variables can be controlled and measured, as with chemistry or physics.
- Open systems cannot control all variables and so prediction levels are uncertain. This happens in medicine, meteorology and seismology.

Arguments for sociology as a science

The following perspectives maintain that it is possible for sociology to be viewed as a scientific discipline.

Positivism

- For Comte and Durkheim, sociology was a positivistic science as it is the analysis of social facts.
- The use of methods of the natural sciences allows social scientists to look for causation and the social laws governing social behaviour.
- Although Popper argued that sociological theory, especially Marxism, could not be scientific as it was incapable of being falsified, Popperian assumptions have been challenged by more recent philosophers of science.

Marxism

Marx claimed that his theory of the development of capitalism was scientific as it was testable to a degree (the law of capital).

Kaplan

- Sociology can be seen to operate reconstructed logics and logics in use, so it is as scientific or as unscientific as the natural sciences.
- Reconstructed logics in sociology depend on the subjective interpretation of meaning.

Realism

- There are many similarities between sociology and other sciences as both are concerned with observable phenomena and the (invisible) underlying structures and processes. However, realist theories cannot be tested as they are not in a positivistic sense testable.
- Durkheim used what is now recognised as a realist approach in his analysis of suicide by examining meanings of religious/family membership etc. as well as structural factors.

Arguments against sociology as a science

Interpretivism

- The subject matter of sociology differs fundamentally from that of the natural sciences. People cannot be studied using controlled observation.
- Individuals have consciousness and free will and are not passive recipients of external forces. Motivation and meaning must be taken into account to gain a valid understanding of social action.
- However, as Becker has argued, it is possible for interactionist research methods to be as systematic as more quantitative methods. Coding schedules can be used for secondary data and clear guidelines produced for conducting participant observation.

Kuhn

- Sociology is not scientific as it is pre-paradigmatic.
- However, Kuhn has overestimated the amount of consensus between natural scientists.
- He fails to examine the competitive nature of the scientific community.
- Many natural sciences are also multi-paradigmatic.
- Positivistic sociology may claim to be scientific but is merely an ideological approach.

Feminism

- Sociology must produce interpretative understandings using in-depth methods and therefore positivist methods are inappropriate.
- Sociologists should be able to relate to respondents, gain their trust and even reciprocate with information etc.
- However, some feminists argue that research should use all available methods but care should be taken to avoid sexist attitudes and assumptions.

Conclusion

The debate around the scientific nature of sociology still rages. It seems that both natural science and social science have aims in common — they attempt to produce models and/or theories that explain the natural or social world as objectively as possible on the basis of the best evidence available at present.

Sociology and value-freedom

Part of the debate around the scientific nature of sociology is the idea that scientists operate with objectivity and value-freedom. This means that researchers' values and opinions are detached from their results and that their beliefs and desires should not enter the research and/or prejudice the results. It is a central tenet of the positivist approach to research.

Arguments for value-freedom in sociology

Many of the early social thinkers believed that sociology should and could be value-free.

Positivism

Positivists such as Comte and Durkheim believed that the application of scientific methodology would achieve this. As positivism saw sociology as scientific, sociologists must also be value-free as their results can be verified against other social facts.

Max Weber

- Weber was less sure that value-freedom was possible, although he maintained that when the topic for research was chosen, it was possible for the researcher to be objective.

- He accepted a scientific approach generally, but as he stressed the uniqueness of historical events, he rejected the possibility of social laws governing behaviour.
- For him, individuals view the world from a value-laden perspective, so the value position of the sociologist will affect the choice of what will be investigated. This is **value-relevance**.
- The selection of a research area will frequently reflect contemporary issues and concerns.
- It is possible for sociologists to take values as a topic of investigation to see how they change over time.

Arguments against value-freedom in sociology

Other sociologists argue that sociology cannot or should not be value-free.

Gunnar Myrdal

- Objectivity is an ideal to strive for, but is unachievable.
- All scientists are prone to bias, but more so in social science because social scientists are part of the subject matter they study.
- Sociologists should make their value position clear when they present their findings.

Interpretivists

- The idea of sociology as a social enterprise possibly being value-free is inconceivable.
- To choose a subject of study is to express a value position.

Gouldner

- Sociologists actually commit themselves to domain assumptions and these affect their perceptions and the way that research is conducted.
- Facts cannot be separated from values in research.
- Sociologists should be open about their personal values so that others can decide how objective they have been.

Becker

- Social scientists cannot maintain value freedom.
- He believes that social researchers should declare 'whose side they are on' — this is likely to be the anti-establishment side, aligned with the 'underdog'.

Whose side are sociologists on?

Marxism

- Marxism starts from the assumption that there are social inequalities and conflicts of interest, which it then seeks to analyse.
- Marx was theoretically and politically committed to revolutionary change and this influenced his analysis of capitalist development.

Functionalism

- Functionalism supports the status quo. It is essentially a conservative position opposed to revolutionary change.
- Functionalists do not interrogate power interests, so they are seen as ideologically conservative.

Feminism

Although there are some ideological differences between the various feminist approaches, in general they assume that social and political inequalities are created by patriarchal institutions.

New Right

- This is a post-functionalist approach committed to abolition of the welfare state.
- New Right theorists view poverty as the fault of individuals.
- They are supporters of what they see as traditional morality and desire more social control over disruptive elements.

Values and research

It is inevitable that values enter the work of sociologists at the theoretical level as well as at all stages of the research process.

- Funding of projects might create obligations to the funding body, which might lead to data bias.
- The choice of topic is affected by the value-relevance of the researcher. Anti-racists undertake research on race issues; feminists undertake research on gender issues.
- The level of involvement of the researcher depends on the method chosen.
- The interpretation of data is affected by the sociological community, as schools of thought create different perspectives for sociologists. Data will be interpreted within certain frameworks.

- Dissemination to whom and where will also involve values. A study on a deviant group might be both helpful to the establishment and detrimental to the interests of the group studied.

Sociology and social policy

Social policy and sociology are sometimes confused by those outside the discipline.

Social policy

Social policy refers to those policies produced by governments that are concerned with social welfare. Thus policies that affect families, health, social security and the social services come under this umbrella. Policies affecting employment and education are also involved.

Sociology

- Sociology is linked to social policy, but is also quite separate from it. Sociologists may often act as government advisers on social policy decisions. They have the necessary expertise to apply appropriate theories and research methodologies to the problem under investigation. This provides evidence on which policy decisions may be made.
- It is possible for sociologists to inform governments on the potential outcomes of new policies. When new policy is proposed, sociologists can research the possible impact on the public and relay this information to governments. Whether governments act on their advice is a matter for empirical investigation.
- Sociological research has been commissioned on many social welfare areas such as race relations, poverty and education.

Positivist and interpretivist approaches to research

These approaches influence the methodology that sociologists use in undertaking research, although they may not be the most important influence, as we shall see later.

Positivism

Positivists assume that sociological explanations should be like those of natural sciences, and that sociologists should use the logic, methods and procedures of natural science. Positivism is more generally associated with structuralist approaches in sociology.

Assumptions

- Social reality is an objective entity capable of being measured by using scientific methods.
- As with the natural world, social behaviour is governed by underlying causal laws and is therefore predictable.
- By systematic observation of causal relationships between social phenomena, these laws can be revealed.
- An example of the discovery of causal laws can be seen in Durkheim's work on suicide, where he showed that the laws of moral regulation and social integration affected an individual's likelihood of suicide.

Sociological approaches
functionalism; Marxism; feminism

Evaluation
+ A positivist approach sees sociology as a scientific discipline.
+ It allows us to examine the nature of external constraints.
- Individuals have subjective consciousness and their behaviour is not easily predictable.
- Positivism does not allow for the possibility of examining the meaning of social actions.
- There is more than one social reality.

Interpretivism

- Interpretivism developed from the work of Weber and the early Chicago School — Dewey, Cooley, Thomas and Mead.
- Weber's verstehen sociology emphasised the meaning of social action as understood by the social actors involved.
- Mead emphasised the concept of self in understanding social action.

Assumptions

- The subject matter of sociology is fundamentally different from that of natural sciences.

- The subjective consciousness of individuals cannot be quantified.
- There is no possibility of gaining understanding of social action through scientific methods.
- Social meanings are the most important aspect of interaction and these need to be understood by sociologists using qualitative methods.
- There are no causal laws governing social behaviour.
- An example of this approach can be seen in Goffman's work on total institutions, in which he showed how inmates construct practices to 'make out' in the institution.

Sociological approaches

phenomenology; social action; symbolic interactionism; feminism; verstehen sociology

Evaluation

+ Interpretivism allows us to see that individuals perceive social reality in different ways.
+ It gives agency to individuals — they are not seen as simply manipulated by external forces.
- The methods used tend to be unsystematic and rely on the subjectivity of the researcher.
- It fails to examine the effects of structured relationships on individuals, especially power differences.
- It underestimates the extent of patterned regularities in society.

Links to methods

These approaches are linked with specific types of method in research.

Positivist sociologists see social reality as objective and measurable, and tend to favour quantitative methods such as social surveys using postal or self-administered questionnaires and/or structured interviews. They sometimes, but rarely, undertake laboratory experiments and make use of official statistics as secondary data. Content analysis of the media is usually quantitative.

Interpretivist sociologists see social reality as constructed through the meanings of social action and tend to favour qualitative methods such as participant observation, unstructured interviews and field experiments. With secondary data, they are more likely to examine personal documents and descriptive historical documents. Content analysis of the media is qualitative and semiology may be used.

However, sociologists are increasingly making use of **methodological pluralism** — using several methods in one research project. This enhances validity, reliability and generalisability.

SOCIOLOGICAL METHODS

We turn now to examine the methods that sociologists use in undertaking their investigations.

- Methods can be **quantitative**, in which case they produce numerical and statistical data, or **qualitative**, where in-depth, meaning-rich data are gained.
- They can also be divided into **primary** methods of data collection, where researchers collect the data themselves, and **secondary** methods, where the data have been collected by another for a purpose other than the present research. Primary and secondary data can be both quantitative and qualitative.
- **Primary data** are collected through **social surveys** using questionnaires and/or interviews; **experiments** including laboratory and field, or by use of the **comparative method** if the experiment is not possible; and **observation**, including non-participant and participant observation.
- **Secondary data** can take the form of quantitative evidence such as **official statistics** or more qualitative evidence, such as **personal documents** (e.g. letters, diaries and photographs) and **historical documents** (e.g. parish records). It is possible for earlier sociologists' work to be used as secondary data. **Content analysis** of mass media material can be both quantitative and qualitative.

Primary research methods
Sampling techniques

When undertaking research, sociologists have to select an appropriate sample of the research population. Almost all research involves this process, and the type of sample chosen may have important consequences for the reliability of the data collected.

There are several different kinds of sampling procedure, some of which are more representative than others.

Random sampling

In random sampling, each person or unit has an equal chance of being selected. At its simplest, it is a 'picking out of a hat' method. More sophisticated techniques involve random number tables. Simple random sampling will not produce representative samples — for instance, choosing a sample of schoolchildren by random means is very unlikely to produce numbers of girls and boys in the same proportion as they exist in the school.

Stratified random sampling

This technique is more representative, as it divides the research population into specific groups or strata and then randomly selects a sample from each group in the same proportion as they exist in the population.

Quota sampling

This is usually the method of market research and opinion polls. An interviewer is given a quota of interviews to conduct with individuals fulfilling specific characteristics. The sample is not random as the choice of interviewees lies with the interviewer. Individuals with the same social characteristics do not have an equal chance of being selected.

Multistage sampling

This provides a cheaper and quicker alternative to actual random samples. It involves different stages, at each of which the samples are subdivided. It may be used for opinion polls where constituencies are chosen and then samples are drawn from them.

Snowball sampling

This is used only in cases where there is no sampling frame. It needs personal contacts to pass on informants to the researcher. It is particularly useful with deviant groups, where initial contact with one person can build up further contacts, who can then bring in even more.

Volunteer sampling

This is similar to snowball sampling, but the researcher may advertise or leaflet in order to gain contacts. This is what Milgram did for his obedience to authority experiments.

Each of these methods has its advantages and disadvantages. In choosing a technique, much depends upon the nature of the research being carried out.

Social surveys

Social surveys are the most popular social research method because they can gather a great deal of data from a large section of the population in a relatively short time. They frequently use the pre-coded questionnaire; however, some social surveys can also be carried out through interviews.

Ackroyd and Hughes (1981) distinguish between three types of survey:

(1) Factual — the government census is a factual survey, as it collects descriptive data.

(2) Attitude — opinion polls come into this category, as they collect people's attitudes to events and issues.

(3) Explanatory — these are more sociological as they are used to test hypotheses and produce new theories.

Questionnaires

A questionnaire is a pre-set, pre-coded list of standardised questions given to a respondent. If the questionnaire is read out by an interviewer, it becomes a structured interview (see below).

Postal questionnaires are mailed to respondents, usually with a stamped addressed envelope or some small incentive to return the form.

Questionnaires produce a large amount of quantitative data and can be given to a large sample of the population.

Questions can be open-ended, which gives the respondent an opportunity to expand answers, or closed/fixed-choice, where the respondent has limited choices.

Evaluation

+ The data collected by questionnaire is seen by positivist researchers as being highly reliable and objective.
+ There is little personal involvement on the part of the researcher after the initial construction of the questionnaire.
+ Large quantities of data can be produced, and quickly and easily analysed by computer.
+ They can be used to test hypotheses, indicate social trends and make predictions of future trends.
+ They are regarded as scientific by government agencies and opinion pollsters.
+ Postal questionnaires can be sent to a very wide sample.
- Interpretivist sociologists criticise the questionnaire for the way the researcher's constructs are imposed on the respondent. They also argue that they are inadequate devices for discovering the meanings and motivations of social behaviour.
- It may not be the case that different answers actually reflect real differences, as respondents may be interpreting questions in different ways.
- They can be too inflexible for respondents, who are limited to answering only the questions asked.
- Validity may be low as a result of misunderstanding, dishonesty or embarrassment.

- Postal questionnaires have their own problems, such as a low response rate, a possible lack of representativeness among those responding and the inability to check who has completed the form.
- If more qualitative data are collected, the researcher has to create categories in order to analyse them, which again involves second-order constructs.

Examples of studies using questionnaires

- **Peter Townsend** (1979) administered questionnaires so that he could measure the extent of poverty in the UK.
- **Shere Hite** (1988) sent out postal questionnaires to 100,000 women in the USA to ask them about their sexual behaviour. Her book is based on 4,500 replies. These replies cannot be taken as representative of American women's views.

Interviewing

Three kinds of interview are used by sociologists: structured, semi-structured and unstructured interviews. All interviews involve a face-to-face interaction between an interviewer and an interviewee. They range from highly formal to a relaxed conversation. The length of the interview varies greatly.

Structured interviews

These are pre-coded questionnaires (interview schedule), where standardised closed questions are asked by the interviewer of all interviewees. This approach is often used for market research. The quantitative data produced are easily collated and analysed by computer.

Unstructured interviews

In contrast, unstructured interviews are in-depth and non-standardised, and rapport and trust are built up over a longer period of time. This approach is flexible, uses openended questions and gives the interviewees more freedom to express their views. This qualitative method is often adopted by interpretivist and feminist researchers.

Semi-structured interviews

This approach combines the advantages of both structured and unstructured interviews. The researcher can access data from standardised questions and the interviewee is able to elaborate where necessary, thus producing both quantitative and qualitative data.

Evaluation

+ Validity is likely to be high with semi- and unstructured interviews, whereas reliability is higher with structured interviews.

+ The response rate for all interviews is much higher than with postal or self-administered questionnaires.

+ Interviewers can explain misunderstandings to the interviewee and prompt where necessary.

+ Feminists argue that unstructured interviews enable researchers to develop a more equal relationship with their subjects. Oakley used this approach with women on the labour ward in her book *From Here to Maternity*.

+ Natural settings are more likely to put interviewees at ease and help to produce more valid findings.

− Interviewer bias: the interviewer's presence will inevitably affect the interviewee. Social characteristics of the interviewer, such as gender, ethnicity and accent, will affect responses from the interviewee.

− Cost: interviews are likely to cost more then self-administered questionnaires and for this reason fewer are undertaken, making the results less representative.

− Artificiality of the situation: the constraints of a formal interview are likely to reduce the validity of the data collected.

− Semi- and unstructured interviews necessitate the imposition of second-order constructs (the researcher's own categorisation and interpretation of data). This again reduces the validity of the data.

Examples of studies using interviews

Structured interviews: Young and Willmott, The Symmetrical Family (1975)

Young and Willmott's work on the history of the family led them to argue that there had been three distinct stages in the history of the family, and to predict a future fourth type. In the 1970s they conducted a social survey using structured interviews in Greater London, asking couples about the division of labour in the home. From their results they claimed that there was now greater equality between men and women in marriage. We were witnessing the development of the egalitarian marriage. However, their research was severely criticised by feminists for its methodology.

Unstructured interviews: Dobash and Dobash, Violence against Wives (1980)

The study was based on unstructured interviews with 109 women who had reported domestic violence to the police. Dobash and Dobash argued that this approach was the most appropriate because the subject matter of the research was very sensitive. They wanted to validate the women's experiences and let women speak for themselves. Their research on domestic violence led them to argue that: 'The fact is that for most people, and especially women and children, the family is the most violent group to which they are likely to belong. Despite fears to the contrary it is not a stranger but a so-called loved one who is most likely to assault, rape or murder us.'

Semi-structured interviews: Charlotte Butler, Young Women and Islam (1995)

Butler conducted 30 semi-structured interviews with young Muslim women in Britain to discover their relationship with their faith. Her research showed that Islam was an important and positive force in their lives. Their religion provided them with a strong sense of identity and her research contradicted stereotypes about the oppressive nature of religion on young Muslim women.

Experiments — laboratory and field

The experiment is the classic research method of the natural sciences. It is the means by which hypotheses are empirically tested according to the hypothetico-deductive model. Experiments involve the manipulation of an independent variable (cause) and the observation of a dependent variable (effect), whilst controlling extraneous variables in order to test a hypothesis.

Laboratory experiments

Laboratory experiments are designed to achieve a rigorous empirical test in which variables are closely controlled and observations and measurements are accurately recorded so that the effect of changing one or more of the variables can be analysed. By rigorous experimentation, the researcher aims to identity cause and effect rather than simply a chance occurrence.

Laboratory experiments have been widely used in psychology to assess the individual's psychological reactions to stimuli. Laboratory experiments in psychology have examined social behaviour under controlled conditions where it is claimed that hypotheses can be tested objectively.

Evaluation

+ The experiment is internally valid if it has been conducted in a rigorous manner. It is then possible that the hypothesis has been proven and that cause and effect has been identified.

+ In the case of Milgram's experiment, we have learned a great deal about obedience and it is possible to understand how individuals have committed atrocities under orders. Similarly, the prison simulation of Zimbardo et al. demonstrated the immediate effects of the prison on inmates and the abuse of power by the guards.

− Although experiments are the classic positivist method, they have limited application in sociology. They are rarely employed for practical, theoretical and ethical reasons.

− Only a limited number of conditions can be simulated in a laboratory, making it impossible to recreate normal life.

− There is always the possibility of demand characteristics and the experimenter effect, where the awareness of being in an experiment affects the behaviour of the person undertaking the experiment.

− Many sociologists would question the ethics of conducting experiments on human beings, especially where they are being deceived about the real nature of the experiment.

Field experiments

Not all experiments on people are carried out in a laboratory. Field experiments test social behaviour in the real world in everyday social contexts. For example, a study of social class conducted on Paddington station compared people's responses to a request for directions when a researcher wore a suit and bowler hat with responses to the same request when he wore labouring clothes.

Examples of studies using experiments

Laboratory experiments

In his study *Obedience to Authority* (1974), **Stanley Milgram** found that 65% of his 40 volunteers were willing to inflict apparently dangerous electric shocks of up to 450 volts on people when instructed to do so by individuals in authority.

Field experiments

- **Honey, Banks and Zimbardo** (1973) studied the effects of allowing students to role-play prisoners and wardens.
- **Mayo** (1933) began the Hawthorne studies in the 1920s with an experiment to test the effects of illumination on productivity.
- **Rosenhan** (1973) sent his researchers into psychiatric hospitals in the USA in the late 1960s to test referral and labelling of schizophrenics. He discovered that it was very easy to be referred to a mental hospital and that, once a person is labelled as mentally ill, it is virtually impossible for them to lose the label.
- **Rosenthal and Jacobson** (1968) in a field experiment used IQ tests to demonstrate the self-fulfilling prophecy.

Participant observation

Participant observation (PO) involves the researcher joining the group which is to be studied and observing social interaction in a natural context. PO is a research method commonly used by ethnographers and social anthropologists. Broadly speaking, the researcher may observe the group with or without the group's knowledge.

- **Covert PO** involves deception — a researcher uses a disguise or lies to the group in order to study it.
- With **overt PO** the group is aware that it is being studied and the researcher's identity is known.

However, in many PO studies the overt/covert line is not so clear cut because the researcher's identity may be known to some but not all of the group's members, or the group may have some idea that the researcher is writing about the area/institution but not necessarily about the group itself.

Evaluation

+ Interpretivists claim that PO produces highly valid data. Social actors are studied in a naturalistic environment and the data are in-depth and detailed.

+ In contrast to survey techniques, the participant observer does not impose his or her definition of reality on those studied. Social actors are allowed to speak for themselves and the researcher's aim is to achieve verstehen — to see the world from the point of view of others.

+ PO may be the only way to gain access to the group. This is likely to be the case with socially deviant groups that would not be identifiable by means of a traditional sampling frame.

+ PO may provide answers to questions that the researcher had not even considered asking.

− Covert PO raises many ethical issues. The group will not have given consent to being observed and its trust will have been broken.

− PO requires the researcher to participate in the group's activities and at the same time to remain detached enough to observe and interpret its behaviour. This is no easy feat. Researchers can become over-involved with the group's activities, stop observing and simply take part. This is known as 'going native'. Data produced are likely to be highly biased and very subjective.

− Positivists reject this qualitative approach because they claim that it is highly unreliable and unscientific. PO studies are impossible to replicate in the same way as survey data. Data produced will inevitably reflect the interests of the researcher and the way events and interactions are interpreted.

− PO is a highly individual technique and requires tremendous skill on the part of the researcher. This is particularly true of covert PO, where the researcher is acting all the time. Role pretence may be a very stressful and dangerous experience for the sociologist who is involved in a group's illegal activity.

− Recording data is a challenging task for the covert researcher. First, researchers cannot risk asking too many direct questions for fear of arousing suspicion. Secondly, they have to find a safe and secure method of recording data. Macintyre used hidden cameras to film his investigations into abuse in residential homes and the fashion industry, while Festinger et al. made repeated visits to the toilet to write up their findings of a cult. Humphreys relied on memory to write up his observations of homosexual encounters. Inevitably the sociologist will forget certain events/conversations and may interpret events in a different way from the group.

− Both joining and leaving the group can be very difficult. The researcher is likely to rely on a disguise or story to gain entry to the group and may have to leave suddenly if under threat.

Examples of studies using participant observation

Laud Humphreys, Tea Room Trade (1970)

Humphreys' aim was to investigate the world of impersonal gay sexual encounters in public toilets across the USA. He wanted to show that straight men were not at risk from unwanted gay advances because they did not understand or participate in the ritual involved in gay encounters. Humphreys acted as a voyeur (look-out) for the men and repeated his observations across the states. He wanted to find out the marital status of those men and identified them through their car registrations. Humphreys then visited them at home under the pretext of conducting a health survey. From the survey data he found out that many of the men were married.

James Patrick, A Glasgow Gang Observed (1973)

Patrick covertly studied a gang of young men in Glasgow. He joined the gang on the invitation of one of its members, Tim, an ex-student of Patrick. He was required to take part in burglaries and observed several fights. The gang was very tough and their violence disturbed Patrick. Although he was known to Tim, he was covert to the rest of the group and he changed his appearance to fit in. Patrick's cover was nearly blown on several occasions when he dressed wrongly, spoke differently and was called 'sir' by Tim out of earshot of the rest. Patrick left the group in a hurry when their violence became too problematic, delayed publication of the study for several years and used a pseudonym.

Sallie Westwood, All Day Everyday: Factory and Family in the Making of Women's Lives (1984)

This is an overt participant observation of women hosiery workers in 'Needletown'. Westwood spent a year visiting the factory and getting to know the women. She observed and interviewed women at work and joined them for nights out on the town. Her study is an illuminating account of the lives of working-class women in the Midlands, combining an ethnographic approach with a feminist analysis of marriage, relationships, family life and work.

Case studies

A case study is 'a detailed in-depth study of one group or event. The group or event is not necessarily representative of others of its kind, and case studies are used as preliminary pieces of research to generate hypotheses for subsequent research' (Lawson and Garrod, *A to Z of Sociology*, 1996). This approach is sometimes referred to as **ethnographic**.

A case study may involve research into a single institution, such as a school or factory, a community or even a family. The aim of a case study is to gain a detailed understanding of the way of life of those observed. A sociologist may combine several methods in the case study but, in general, researchers tend to favour qualitative approaches such as participant observation and unstructured interviewing to gain an in-depth understanding of the group.

Evaluation

+ Case studies provide the sociologist with detailed and valid data.

+ They may serve to challenge and disprove existing assumptions about social groups. For example, the work of Eileen Barker on the Moonies challenged media fears of brainwashing by the sect.
+ The research may act as a springboard for further research in the field.
− The group or institution under study may be atypical and then the results will not be generalisable.
− Case studies are often a highly individual technique and this raises the problem of subjectivity on the part of the researcher.
− The data collected may be valid but not reliable.

Examples of case studies

Paul Willis, Learning to Labour (1977)

Willis's study was based on 12 working-class lads and their experience of education and their first year at work.

Eileen Barker, The Making of a Moonie (1984)

Barker's research involved the use of surveys, unstructured interviews and participant observation over a number of years, examining recruitment patterns and the experience of life as a member of the sect.

Secondary research methods

Quantitative secondary data: official statistics

Official statistics are numerical data produced by both central and local government. They provide a rich source of information for sociologists. Sociologists often differentiate between hard statistics and soft statistics.

Hard statistics are those figures that are seen to be relatively immune to processes of manipulation and bias in their collection, e.g. birth, death, marriage and divorce statistics. Although divorce statistics may not be a particularly valid indicator of unhappiness in marriage in society, they are a completely reliable indicator of the number of divorces because you cannot legally terminate a marriage without becoming a statistic.

In contrast, **soft statistics** are those figures that are prone to subjectivity, bias and manipulation in their collection and presentation. They include data on crime, poverty, unemployment and suicide — aspects of society about which people may make value judgements. It is possible to see that the collection and interpretation of such data may be politically motivated to benefit those in power.

+ Official statistics are very useful to sociologists for identifying trends and making comparisons over time and between countries.
+ They provide the sociologist with a useful source of background data. They save the sociologist vast amounts of time and expense because they are readily available.
+ Positivists see official statistics as 'hard' objective data. For example, the census is sent to every household and therefore the data are highly reliable and representative. This means that generalisations can be made from them about society.
− The data might not be exactly what the sociologist needs because they were collected for another purpose.
− Interpretivists question the validity of official statistics. They see them as the end product of a social process of collection.
− Figures can be subject to manipulation and bias. Marxists would argue that statistics produced by the state tend to reflect the interests of a powerful elite. They might be used to justify the existing social order.
− Feminists argue that many statistics are sexist and reflect malestream research. For example, women's social class has often been assumed to be that of their husband, and women have simply been ignored in much sociological research.

Examples of studies using official statistics

Durkheim, Le Suicide (1897)

Durkheim's classic text *Le Suicide* was an attempt to show that society could be studied in a rigorous and scientific manner. He used European statistics on suicide and compared the rate between countries in the nineteenth century. He wanted to show that suicide was not simply an individual act, but that the suicide rate was a social phenomenon and had to be understood in terms of the society in which it existed.

Dobash and Dobash, Violence against Wives (1980)

Dobash and Dobash used crime statistics as a starting point for their research into domestic violence against women in Scotland. From the interviews they conducted, they found that many women had experienced up to 35 episodes of violence before they reported it to the police. Thus the official picture of domestic violence concealed a significant dark figure of crime.

Qualitative secondary data

In their research, sociologists often use secondary data as background sources, or analyse secondary data to test their own hypotheses. We tend to think of secondary data as only statistical, but there are many other kinds of secondary material available which are qualitative, including letters, oral histories, diaries, biographies, autobiographies, novels, newspapers and other mass media, such as film, television and photography.

Interpretivist sociologists advocate the use of life documents such as letters and diaries in research, because individuals created these documents and reflect on their personal experiences or report their feelings about events in their lives. Interpretivist sociologists aim to achieve verstehen in their work and to understand the meanings and motivations of social actors engaged in social action. Qualitative secondary material is in-depth, often expressive and meaningful. It therefore should enable the researcher to gain a valid insight into the lives of those whom they wish to study.

Evaluation

+ Qualitative secondary data can be invaluable sources of information about current and historical events.
+ They may provide detailed and valid accounts of people's thoughts and feelings at a particular time.
+ They may be the only possible means of understanding the way of life of a group in the past.
+ Life documents offer a richer, more in-depth picture of the way people feel and act than is possible with social surveys and other quantitative approaches.
+ The data can be usefully combined with quantitative approaches to achieve more valid and reliable findings (methodological pluralism and triangulation).
− Life documents may be highly subjective and therefore biased and invalid.
− Autobiographies are inevitably selective and partial. They were written with an audience in mind and often aim to impress the reader.
− Historical documents may not cover the particular period desired.
− Positivists reject the use of these data owing to their lack of reliability.
− As the data have to be interpreted by the researcher, this inevitably introduces the element of subjectivity.

Examples of studies using secondary qualitative data

Thomas and Znaniecki, **The Polish Peasant in Europe and America (1919)**

They made extensive use of a collection of documents, including 764 letters, diaries and newspaper articles, regarding immigration and the arrival and lives of Polish émigrés in Europe and the USA.

Valery Hey, **The Company She Keeps: An Ethnography of Girls' Friendships (1997)**

Valery Hey looked at girls' friendships in two London comprehensives. Her study provides an interesting example of the effective use of secondary qualitative data in research. She combined overt participant observation with the use of notes scribbled in lessons and girls' diaries. The girls in her study had kept their notes and letters for several years and were willing for Hey to use them in her research. She claimed that writing notes was an important part of the girls' friendships, and while teachers saw these notes as 'silliness' and 'garbage', Hey argues that 'they were sociologically fascinating because they were an important means of transmitting the cultural values of friendship'.

Content analysis

Content analysis is the main research method used by researchers of the mass media. It can also be used to examine personal and historical documents. It is a systematic means of classifying and describing the content of the press, television etc. Content analysis can be both quantitative and qualitative, depending on what the researcher is looking for. It can be used to obtain the frequency of a given message or the nature of the message itself.

- **Quantitative content analysis** generates statistical data from a coding schedule, which is a document like a questionnaire that is completed for each newspaper article, television programme or magazine. It can be used to calculate the amount of space given over to events and/or to count the number of times a particular issue or group, or even particular words, occurs.
- **Qualitative content analysis** generates descriptive data and examines the messages and ideological content of the media or of particular documents. It can be used, for example, to look at the messages around gender or ethnic represen-tation in the media by analysing photographs, dialogue, situations etc. This method often takes a semiological approach to texts.

Evaluation

Quantitative content analysis

+ The material is easily available and inexpensive (even free).
+ The data are easily coded and analysed.
+ The method limits the researcher effect, as all coders follow the same schedule.
+ It can be used to monitor recent events and to make comparisons over time.
− The problems of this method are similar to those of the questionnaire, as a coding schedule is used.
− Even though coders may be trained, they may not code the material in the same way.
− Second-order constructs of the researcher may not reflect the way the audience receives the text.
− It does not address the issue of audience reception and may assume passivity.

Qualitative content analysis

+ This method engages the meanings of texts and communications.
+ It can be used to interpret the underlying ideological messages of texts.
− Interpretation is a highly subjective process and individuals perceive things in different ways.
− Researchers rarely check out how the audience interprets the messages of the texts.
− Given the nature of the texts and forms of communication, the data are likely to be unrepresentative.
− By turning qualitative images, words and order on the page into quantitative figures and frequencies, subtlety may be lost.

Examples of studies using content analysis

- **T. A. van Djik** in *Racism in the Press* (1991) examined the coverage of race relations in the press by using both quantitative and qualitative content analysis.
- **The Glasgow Media Group** has used both quantitative and qualitative content analysis in many of its studies, from *Bad News* (1985) to *Message Received* (1999).

Choice of methods

Sociologists face a number of decisions when conducting research. The most important one is which method(s) to choose, but this decision is affected by many other factors. We can divide the factors affecting choice into three: practical, ethical and theoretical. The factor of most significance depends upon the nature of the research.

Practical decisions

- **Funding** This may be the most significant issue for any researcher. So much in research depends on the availability of money — the size of the sample, the time the research can take, the number of research assistants etc. A lone researcher may carry out a study involving participant observation where there is likely to be no external funding, but a research department may be dependent on government funding for a large social survey. Funding bodies may have ownership rights over the research data and they may have power of veto on whether the research findings can be published.
- **Time** This is related to cost and can affect whether several interviews can take place over time or whether only one interview is possible.
- **Access** Without acceptance into the institution or group to be studied, there will be no research. Researchers may be asked to take on a role in return for the access: for example, Willis helped with the youth wing of the school in *Learning to Labour*.

Ethical decisions

- **Moral issues** Apart from maintaining the BSA ethical guidelines, sociologists must be aware of the sensitivity of some areas and the possible impact of their research on respondents. Research is not usually a two-way process and respondents may feel that their trust and friendship have been betrayed.
- **Illegality** Researchers may be called upon to engage in criminal acts or to witness others doing so.
- **Danger** In some cases, researchers may place themselves in danger during their study.
- **After-effects** Some methods, such as experimentation, may have lasting effects on respondents who were misinformed about the nature of the study.

Theoretical decisions

- **Methodological approach** The methodological approach of the researcher is likely to affect the choice of method, with positivists choosing quantitative methods.
- **Theoretical perspective** The theoretical perspective of the researcher — whether Marxist, feminist etc. — will affect the choice of method and the nature of the research.

Questions
&
Answers

This section of the guide provides you with four questions on the topic of **Theory and Methods** in the style of the AQA unit test. The first three questions are followed by grade-A and grade-C responses. It is important to note that the grade-A answers are not 'model' answers — they do not represent the only, or even necessarily the best, way of answering these questions. It would be quite possible to take a different approach, or to use different material, or even to come to a different conclusion, and still gain very high marks. Rather, the answers represent a particular 'style': one that answers the question set and displays the appropriate skills, including using suitable concepts and studies, displaying a critical and evaluative awareness towards the material used, and presenting a logically structured argument. The grade-C responses are candidate answers that are basically on the right track, but which fail, for various reasons, to score very high marks.

A fourth question is provided which is not accompanied by candidate answers, but is left for you to write your own. Some pointers are given to help put you on the right track.

Examiner's comments
The candidate answers are accompanied by examiner's comments. These are preceded by the icon Ⓔ and indicate where credit is due. For the grade-A answers, the examiner shows you what it is that enables the candidates to score so highly. Particular attention is given to the use of the examinable skills: knowledge and understanding, and analysis and evaluation. For the grade-C answers, the examiner points out areas for improvement, specific problems and common errors. You might consider rewriting the answer in order to gain higher marks.

Social surveys; official statistics; structural and Marxist perspectives

Section A

Item A

The National Child Development Study (NCDS) is a longitudinal survey which began with 4,000 children born in one week in March 1958. Follow-up surveys at 16, 23 and 33 have tracked the original group and the data have been widely used to understand the importance of class and education (among other factors) in a person's life. Using NCDS data we know that the sons of professional fathers are much more likely to get professional jobs than sons of working class parents. We also know that working class children who achieve A-level qualifications are far more likely to move up the social scale than their working class friends who leave school with just the odd GCSE.

Source: Hugh Chignell, 'Longitudinal research', S (an A-level sociology magazine), 3 April 1999.

Item B

Different perspectives in sociology tend to become associated with different types of method. Structural perspectives such as functionalism, which see society as a system consisting of interconnected parts, are normally associated with positivist approaches to research. So the researcher is more likely to make use of quantitative methods such as social surveys or, if secondary data are used, official statistics.

However, it is not always so cut and dried. Some researchers who support a structural perspective may use a more interpretivist approach in their research. For example in the classic study *Learning to Labour*, Paul Willis, a Marxist sociologist, analysed the experience of working class lads in the British education system in the 1970s by undertaking an ethnographic study.

(1) (a) **Briefly explain what is meant by a longitudinal survey (Item A).** (2 marks)
   (b) **Identify TWO possible problems associated with longitudinal surveys.** (4 marks)
   (c) **With reference to Item B, give THREE reasons why researchers from structural perspectives tend to favour quantitative methods.** (6 marks)
   (d) **Identify and briefly explain TWO characteristics of Marxism.** (8 marks)

Section B

Answer ONE question from this section.

(2) Assess the usefulness of postal questionnaires as a method of sociological research. (40 marks)

(3) Assess the usefulness of official statistics to sociologists. In your answer refer to at least TWO areas of social life. (40 marks)

■ ■ ■

Answer to question 1: grade-A candidate

(1) (a) A longitudinal survey is different from other surveys because it takes place over intervals of time. The researcher surveys a sample of people by structured interviews or questionnaires and then repeats the method at regular intervals. This approach can measure social changes.

This is an excellent answer and gains full marks. **2/2 marks**

(b) One problem is that if the survey lasts a long time it is very difficult to keep in touch with all the people in the original group, which could affect the representativeness.

Another problem is that as the people in the survey are continually asked questions, they may begin to think about things that they would otherwise have taken for granted, thus possibly becoming different from the non-survey population.

Two possible problems have been clearly identified and the candidate gains full marks. **4/4 marks**

(c) Researchers from structural perspectives would favour quantitative methods because they believe that society is an objective reality and so is measurable and observable. They also use official statistics as secondary data as they see such statistics as predictive of future social trends. Finally, they argue that these methods are more scientific and, therefore, more reliable.

The candidate has produced three appropriate reasons and gains full marks. **6/6 marks**

(d) Marxism is a theory of social change based on social and economic relationships arising from ownership and non-ownership of private property in the means of production. This means that Marxists see societies as conflict-based unlike functionalists who see harmony and value-consensus. Marx argued that social change was an essential part of all social history and the new society was always within the old but revolution had to bring it forward.

Another characteristic of Marxism is that it sees relationships between the workers and the employers as exploitative. The employers under a capitalist system have no choice but to become competitive, otherwise they would fail. However, to be competitive they must make profits and these profits come from the labour of the workers. This surplus value of labour power keeps capitalism going and is essentially exploitative.

📝 These are two correctly identified characteristics that are both clearly explained. Can you think of other characteristics that you could explain?   8/8 marks

(2) Written questionnaires are used in social surveys. They are particularly useful because they can be used to survey a wide range of people. They are cheap — this is because interviewers do not have to be employed. Postal questionnaires are simply written or structured questionnaires which are mailed to a sample of respondents. They are particularly useful in research which covers a wide range of locations. The questions on a questionnaire are pre-coded. This means that responses can be easily analysed and presented graphically. Positivists favour this kind of research as they see measurable data as highly reliable. Information is uncovered in a straightforward way clearly and simply. Questionnaires are useful as they require relatively little involvement from the researcher. Mailed question-naires require the least involvement of the researcher, therefore preventing interviewer effect or bias. However, this can also be disadvantageous as there are no possible means of being guided or prompted when misunderstandings occur as might happen in a structured interview.

📝 This is a thorough introductory paragraph. The candidate has focused the response directly on to postal questionnaires rather than spending unnecessary time on questionnaires in general.

However, there are other disadvantages as well. There is usually a very low response rate (unless, like the census, there is a legal requirement to return the form). The response rate is around 50%, but the first Hite Report on the sexual behaviour of American women was as low as 4%. This means that even if a representative sample had been gathered initially, the response rate would make this invalid. It is likely that those who return the forms have a particular point to make or even 'axe to grind', making their responses less likely to be representative.

📝 Appropriate reference is made to disadvantages. The candidate identifies specific studies to demonstrate the problems. The material on Hite is usefully employed.

Other problems include the possibility of an unknown person completing the form or it being sent to someone who is illiterate. There are of course problems general to questionnaires which are also pertinent to those mailed, but they may well be made more difficult by the lack of a researcher as guide.

Interpretivists would reject the idea of using any questionnaire because such tools cannot access the real meaning of the situation as perceived by the individuals involved. They believe that questionnaires simply obtain superficial data and cannot produce the meanings which underlie social action. Feminists would also be critical. Anne Oakley criticised questionnaire research and structured interviews for being too 'malestream' — she argued that the researcher needed to build up trust with the respondent. This is not at all possible with a postal questionnaire.

e This paragraph introduces the theoretical critiques from the interpretivists. Although it is correct, we might have hoped for some development here. The critique from feminists is sound and well focused.

Overall there are many reasons why researchers and especially market researchers would defend the postal questionnaire, but if the researcher is aiming for a rigorous systematic method to produce highly reliable and valid data, the mailed questionnaire has too many drawbacks.

e The candidate has written a reasonable concluding paragraph with good evaluation present. The idea of market research is introduced, but this might have appeared earlier in the essay with some expansion. AO1: 15/20; AO2: 15/20 = 30/40 marks

e **This candidate has produced some very sophisticated responses and clearly has considerable depth and breadth of understanding of sociological theories and concepts. There is pleasing evidence of evaluation and analysis here.**

Overall: 50/60

■ ■ ■

Answer to question 1: grade-C candidate

(1) (a) An example of a longitudinal survey is *7 UP* — a Granada TV programme which followed 7-year-olds from the 1960s to the present day.

e This answer does not define the concept, but gives an example of a longitudinal survey and so gains 1 mark. 1/2 marks

(b) As the survey goes on, some people might not want to carry on with it and may drop out. Another problem is that the method costs a great deal of money.

e These are two appropriate problems and gain full marks. 4/4 marks

(c) In Item B it says that structural perspectives such as functionalism see society as a system and take a positivist approach and use quantitative methods.

e The candidate has simply paraphrased material from Item B and has not shown understanding. Think of ways in which the material could have been used in order to gain marks. 0/6 marks

(d) Marxists see two social classes in society — the bourgeoisie and the proletariat — and the bourgeoisie exploit the proletariat. The proletariat do not understand that they are being exploited.

e The candidate has identified two characteristics but with no explanations. Marks scored = 2 + 0, 2 + 0. 4/8 marks

(3) Official statistics are figures collected by governments for understanding different parts of society. They can be very useful to sociologists. Official statistics can save the sociologists a lot of time and money. Durkheim used statistics in his study of suicide. He looked at statistics from different countries and found out that suicide rates were different in each country but stayed the same over time.

This is a reasonable definition, but the candidate does not take the opportunity to expand on the advantages.

Durkheim wanted to show that suicide was not just an individual act but it was caused by the society the individual lived in. He found four different types of suicide. These were called egoistic, anomic, fatalistic and altruistic. He believed that the suicide statistics were true. However, interactionists such as Jack Douglas have criticised Durkheim for not taking into account the meaning of suicide. For example, he said that some families, especially Roman Catholics, would hide a suicide death because it is a sin. And a suicide could also be seen as an accident if it is a road crash.

The material on Durkheim could be better used to demonstrate the reason for his reliance on statistics. The interactionist critique only implicitly criticises statistics.

Positivists use official statistics because they think social reality is measurable and you can get trends and patterns from official statistics. Other kinds of statistics that sociologists use are crime statistics. These show that the typical offender is a young working-class male. However, this may not be the whole truth. Statistics can be quite dangerous for sociologists because they have a 'dark figure' which is unknown, so some crimes are unreported or unrecorded like white collar crime, so the figures are not accurate. This makes it very difficult to produce accurate theories of crime. However, some of the early sociologists like Cohen and Miller used them to build their theories, but they did not take into account that there were other criminals besides working-class boys — like white collar workers who rarely get counted in the statistics.

There is some relevant material here. The point about incomplete statistics affecting theory building is sound but needs discussion.

So in conclusion we can see that statistics are useful for sociologists but must be used 'with a pinch of salt'.

This conclusion does not really conclude the essay helpfully. However, there is some limited evaluation here.   AO1: 12/20; AO2: 10/20 = 22/40 marks

This candidate has produced fair responses. There is reasonable knowledge and understanding, but the answer is somewhat unsophisticated at times. More emphasis on analysis and evaluation skills would improve the total score.   Overall: 31/60

question 2

Official statistics; multiple methods; feminism; science and sociology

Section A

Item A

Official statistics consist of any statistical data collected and produced by government departments which relate to a specific society. For instance the 2001 census will produce a wide-ranging picture of households in Britain today together with any changes evident from the 1991 census. However, there are many different kinds of official statistics including births, marriages and deaths, employment and unemployment figures and crime statistics. It is important for governments to have access to such data as they can generate policies and make predictions about future social needs.

Many sociologists also make use of such statistics, but interpretivists criticise official statistics as they see them simply as **social constructs** and not an accurate reflection of reality.

Item B

Andy Hobson's research examined the evaluations of teacher training courses by trainee teachers and employed four different research methods — questionnaires, interviews, participant observation and the use of secondary data. In his view: 'The term methodological pluralism, like triangulation, refers to the use by the researcher of more than one method of research, but the emphasis is less on the validity of the data than on the building up of a fuller and more comprehensive picture of social life. What this means is that in using more than one method of research we can enjoy the distinct advantages of each method and of the different kinds of data they produce (e.g. both statistical and verbal accounts), and that the advantages of one method might help to compensate for and, at least partially, overcome the limitations of another.'

Source: adapted from Andy Hobson, 'Multiple methods in social research', *Sociology Review*, Vol. 10, No. 2, November 2000.

(1) (a) Explain what is meant by the term 'social construct' (Item A).   (2 marks)
   (b) Give **TWO** reasons why the census is deemed to be highly reliable.   (4 marks)
   (c) With reference to sociological research, explain **THREE** advantages of the
       use of triangulation (Item B) to the researcher.   (6 marks)

(d) The following statement is a hypothesis that could arise from Hobson's research in Item B: 'Trainee teachers have idealised notions of teaching and unrealistic perceptions of classroom management.' Identify and briefly explain TWO ways in which this hypothesis might be tested, giving reasons for your answer.

(8 marks)

Section B

Answer ONE question from this section.

(2) Assess the contribution of feminism to sociological thought.   (40 marks)

(3) Critically evaluate the view that sociology is not a scientific discipline.   (40 marks)

■ ■ ■

Answer to question 2: grade-A candidate

(1) (a) A social construct is anything that is created by the actions of individuals in society. Interpretivists would argue that statistics are social constructs because they are the end product of a social process.

🖉 This is a good response and the candidate has produced an example to make the definition even clearer, although it is not necessary to do this to gain full marks.

2/2 marks

(b) The census is highly reliable because it is collected every ten years and secondly it is a legal requirement that every household completes it, so it has an extremely high response rate.

🖉 This candidate has given two appropriate reasons and therefore gains full marks.

4/4 marks

(c) Eileen Barker's study of *The Making of a Moonie* is a highly effective use of triangulation. Barker combined PO with unstructured interviewing and questionnaires over a period of several years to gain a detailed and in-depth understanding of the Unification Church. This provided reliable data. The qualitative methods that Barker employed enabled her to gain an understanding of the meaning of membership for the members themselves, providing more valid data, and the quantitative approach of the questionnaires allowed her to compare a much wider range of responses and gain a more representative picture of the views of church members.

🖉 The candidate has identified an appropriate study and identified three strengths of using triangulation — an in-depth understanding of the Unification Church, an understanding of the meaning of membership for those involved, and a comparison of a wider range of responses. The student gains full marks for this answer.

6/6 marks

(d) The first way in which the hypothesis might be tested could be a social survey using structured interviews. Samples would be taken from teachers in their first year of teaching and compared with teachers with at least five years of teaching experience. The reason for this would be to identify any differences between the two groups and to find out whether the trainee teachers share similar perceptions of teaching and classroom management. Positivists would choose this method because they see surveys as highly reliable and more likely to give representative views. The second method would be to use unstructured interviews with teachers at the beginning of their first year in teaching and then repeat the interviews at the end of the year. This would tell you whether their views had changed as a result of their experiences. This is a qualitative approach preferred by interpretivists as it is likely to give valid data because the teachers have the chance to talk for themselves.

This is a very full answer that tests the hypothesis adequately and therefore gains full marks. Can you think of two other ways in which you could test this hypothesis? 8/8 marks

(3) There is much debate in sociology as to whether the subject is scientific. Early sociologists were very concerned that sociology should be recognised as a scientific discipline and should adopt the methods of the natural sciences. However, more recently the nature of science itself has been challenged.

This is a good introduction which identifies that there is a debate about this issue, makes reference to 'early sociologists' and briefly touches on a more recent aspect of the debate.

For example, Lynch's experiments revealed that the 'scientific' method to which the likes of Comte and Durkheim aspired was actually not characteristic of science in general. Kuhn also challenged the objectivity of science when he claimed that science passed through paradigmatic shifts which were similar to ideologies or 'perspectives' in sociological terms. Thus scientists interpreted findings in terms of these belief systems rather than with reference to the qualities inherent in the object of study. We can make a similar point with regard to Popper. The claim to discover objective laws is unscientific irrespective of the subject matter — it is simply impossible. The realist conception of science, as developed by Urry and Sayer, also indicates that in order to be 'scientific' a subject does not have to confine itself to the observable. Natural scientists do not, as viruses and magnetic fields are invisible. Nor is it imperative to manipulate all variables in a controlled environment (seismologists cannot do this). Thus we see that the extent to which sociology can be a scientific discipline depends upon the characteristics with which science is defined.

This is an interesting way of answering the question. The candidate takes on the debate as to whether natural science is as scientific as it claims by referring to problems with the scientific method, paradigm shifts and the realist position.

However, interpretive criticisms often still apply even when we consider science in terms of its realist conception — individuals, unlike matter, have consciousness and our actions can never be completely predicted. Ethnomethodologists and phenomenologists go even further. They maintain that science shows how one thing elicits a response but in society the true nature of external objects can never be known — we all perceive, experience and interpret them differently. Thus external objects or events do not cause humans to act in a certain way — our meaningful interpretations do. No two actions are ever the same.

This candidate demonstrates a sophisticated understanding of the interpretivist position and also makes distinctions between different interpretivist positions.

However, these extreme views against sociology as a science ultimately have to be rejected. Some parts of society do exist and they do have an effect upon us. Poverty and discrimination clearly affect individuals. As some sociologists claim, these things can be measured scientifically and in fact should be, so that society becomes aware of them and hence change may be produced.

Simply because science does not stick rigidly to these aims does not mean that sociology should not. If we interpret science as a rigorous discipline striving for objectivity, then sociology can meet these criteria. There are those who would argue that sociology cannot be value-free. For example, feminists criticise the malestream nature of much sociology, but they also argue that measures should be taken to ensure accuracy. The subjective state of individuals should be taken into account.

It is interesting to see that this candidate has come down on the side of sociology being scientific. It is important to remember that you can take a particular position and, provided that you can support it with arguments and evidence, you will be rewarded.

In conclusion, sociology should and can follow the procedural rigour associated with science, yet this should not be called 'scientific'. Science studies areas of life where actions are meaningless, as they operate without consciousness, whereas individuals are active, sentient and interpretive. This does not rule out the possibility of making causal connections, as some external stimuli such as disease, pollution and poverty affect individuals regardless of how they are interpreted.

This candidate shows a good grasp of the debate. It is surprising, though, that we do not see any reference to a postmodernist approach to the question of science. It would be good practice for you to be familiar with the postmodernist argument. It has become a prominent issue in contemporary sociology.

AO1: 18/20; AO2: 16/20 = 34/40 marks

This candidate has a very sound grasp of the topic and achieves a high-level A grade.   **Overall: 54/60**

■ ■ ■

Answer to question 2: grade-C candidate

(1) (a) A social construct is something that is made by society, not naturally given.

> This is a brief answer, but the candidate has referred to the term 'made' and so is given credit. **2/2 marks**

(b) The census is highly reliable because the answers must be truthful. The law says that you must answer all questions truthfully and therefore it is highly reliable.

> This candidate has made a very common mistake in confusing reliability with validity and therefore does not score any marks. Make sure that you are very clear about the differences between these two important concepts. **0/4 marks**

(c) Laud Humphreys' study of 'tearooms' allowed him to gain access to watching men engage in homosexual encounters. He used covert participant observation so that he could gain an understanding of their behaviour, but he also took their car registration numbers. He had a friend in the police who gave him names and addresses for the men and so Humphreys was able to include them in a survey on men's health. These two methods gave him more data and he was able to find out whether the men were married or not from the survey. This helps to make his data more reliable.

> This candidate implicitly refers to the concept of triangulation and correctly identifies an appropriate study. In order to have gained full marks the candidate needed to discuss another advantage. **4/6 marks**

(d) Group interviews would be a good way to test this hypothesis because they are cheap to carry out and the interviewees are more likely to feel at ease and therefore talk more freely. Weber believed in trying to gain verstehen. This means that you are trying to stand in the shoes of another person and really see the world through their eyes.

> The candidate correctly identifies group interviews to test the hypothesis, but the material on Weber is poorly applied and not well focused. The candidate makes no reference to teaching. 2 + 2 and 0 + 0. **4/8 marks**

(2) There are three main branches of feminism — liberal, Marxist and radical. One of the main liberal feminists was Anne Oakley. She was very interested in the fact that women did housework and they were unpaid. She criticised Young and Willmott because they said that the family was symmetrical. In their study there was only one question about domestic chores and if the husband had done the washing up once a week the relationship was seen to be equal. We know that women in the home still do almost all the housework as well as looking after children and working outside the home. This is called the 'triple shift'.

> This candidate has a reasonably good understanding of liberal feminism and has illustrated the approach by using Oakley's work. However, an opportunity to show more analysis and evaluation has been missed.

Liberal feminists believe that society ought to be more equal and they believe that the law can bring about change. They are in favour of equal opportunities and are against sexism in school and in the workplace. Today girls' levels of achievement are higher than boys' in school and some sociologists argue that this is because of feminism and gender policies in education.

2 This paragraph scores for its extension of the characteristics of liberal feminism. The point about educational achievement is focused on the contribution of feminism, which is the question asked.

Radical feminists are very different from liberal feminists. They see that society is patriarchal and that men have all the power. Radical feminists argue that the family is a very dangerous place for women. Dobash and Dobash showed that domestic violence is common and it is mainly women who are the victims. Radical feminists believe that women should be separate from men and many of them are lesbian separatists — this tends to give them a bad image in the press. Andrea Dworkin said that 'pornography is the theory, rape is the practice'.

2 The essay is out of balance, as this final paragraph on radical feminism is rather too brief. It does make some useful descriptive points and the candidate demonstrates a fair understanding. Although the candidate refers to three branches of feminism, the essay does not examine Marxist feminism. This oversight fails to gain more marks. Overall, the essay is not as well focused on the title as it could be.   AO1: 12/20; AO2: 11/20 = 23/40 marks

2 **The candidate has produced a brief response. Even under the timed conditions of the examination, more is expected of students at A2. This is reflected in the overall mark. The candidate generally shows a fair understanding of sociological material. The essay could have scored more highly if it did not contain some errors of understanding.**   **Overall: 33/60**

Social surveys; science and sociology; positivism; postmodernism

Section A

Item A

Opinion polls and surveys are probably the best known and most widely publicised form of sociological research. Their assumed reliability and scientific validity has endowed them with greater authority than many alternative data-gathering techniques. Political parties, business and commercial organisations and even government departments such as the Home Office invest both large sums of money and considerable faith in the results of surveys. This has meant that survey results carry significant weight — even serving as a justification for stronger criminal justice policies.

Source: Stephen Sinclair, 'Questioning surveys', *Sociology Review*, Vol. 8, No. 2, November 1999.

Item B

Positivism applies the logic, methods and procedures of the natural sciences to the study of society with little modification, but sociology rarely produces results that are as precise and repeatable as those produced by natural scientists (although this is not seen as a major problem by positivists), because sociologists are unable to control all the variables in the situations they study in the way that natural scientists are able to do in their laboratories. Nevertheless, many sociologists have argued that the procedures of the natural sciences can and should be applied to the study of society.

Source: Ken Browne, 'Sociology and science', *Sociology Review*, Vol. 9, No. 3, February 2000.

(1) (a) **With reference to Item B, explain what is meant by 'variables'.** (2 marks)

    (b) **Explain the differences between 'reliability' and 'scientific validity' (Item A).** (4 marks)

    (c) **With reference to Item B, briefly describe three major characteristics of positivism.** (6 marks)

    (d) **Identify and briefly explain TWO problems associated with using the laboratory method as a means to understand social behaviour.** (8 marks)

Section B

Answer ONE question from this section.

(2) Assess the usefulness of different types of observation in sociological research. (40 marks)

(3) Assess the view of postmodernists that metanarratives or 'big stories' are no longer able to make sense of our changing world. (40 marks)

■ ■ ■

Answer to question 3: grade-A candidate

(1) (a) A variable is something which can be measured such as age, gender, income etc. There are independent and dependent variables.

🖉 This is an appropriate response and gains full marks. 2/2 marks

(b) Reliability is the extent to which a study is repeatable and can gain the same results. Scientific validity means that the study actually measures what it sets out to measure.

🖉 The candidate has explained the differences between the two concepts and gains full marks. 4/4 marks

(c) Item A says that positivism is the application of scientific methods to sociological research. This means that it assumes that sociology is a scientific discipline.

Positivists argue that social scientists can be objective in conducting their research and, therefore, do not let their own values and prejudices enter the research.

They see the role of the sociologists as searching for laws which govern social behaviour in the same way that natural laws govern behaviour in the natural world. They also believe that social behaviour is observable and can be measured, so they use quantitative methods in their research studies.

🖉 The candidate clearly understands positivism and has successfully identified more than three characteristics. In this case they are all correct. If you are unsure of three characteristics, don't be afraid to add a further one because you will not be penalised for identifying more than is required. 6/6 marks

(d) We can see problems associated with using the laboratory method as a means of understanding social behaviour by using Milgram's classic experiment *Obedience to Authority*, which has become renowned for its ethical issues. He aimed to find out how far the average American citizen would go in hurting another individual when taking orders from a person in authority. This experiment involved considerable deception on his part. The volunteers thought that they were taking part in a simple learning experiment, but once in the lab they were involved in delivering electric shocks that seemed to be inflicting considerable pain on the learner. We do not know to what extent they followed the orders of the teacher simply because they were in the laboratory, and even when Milgram tested this out by taking the experiment to the high street, it was yet another artificial situation. So their behaviour in these experimental situations cannot be used as evidence of what they would do in an everyday situation.

Another problem is whether it is possible to isolate and control variables of social behaviour. Individuals have consciousness and when they are put in a laboratory they may often produce demand characteristics. Their behaviour may simply be a reflection of what they think the experimenter wants from them. This again cannot be seen as relevant to actual social reality.

> ⭐ Here is a very sophisticated answer. The candidate uses the study to identify two problems associated with the laboratory method in understanding social behaviour, and gains full marks. What other problems can you think of relating to laboratory experiments?   8/8 marks

(2) Observation is mainly adopted by interpretive theorists who seek to understand the micro view of the social world. There are two main types of observation: participant and non-participant. In the first case, the researcher takes part in the action and this may be either covertly or overtly. In the second, the researcher may use unobtrusive methods like cameras to watch the action, or may engage in classroom observation and sit in a classroom taking notes.

> ⭐ This is a good introductory paragraph. The candidate has contextualised observation studies and given two different types of observation.

Participant observation is usually small scale and this has the advantage of providing richer, more in-depth material. Whether the observer is overt or covert, the meanings of the social action can be gained and this is the aim of interpretivist research. In addition the data produced are higher in validity as the researcher is there as action takes place. There is less validity with, for example, structured interviews where interviewer effect can impact on the situation. Terry Williams' study of cocaine dealers in New York from 1982–86 is an example of a study high in validity. He was able to become part of the events which occurred and gained first-hand knowledge.

> ⭐ This paragraph scores for its good focus on usefulness and for its reference to relevant research.

There is also an element of practicality. By becoming a covert observer the researcher gains access to the group which would probably be denied otherwise. For James Patrick, access to the gang was given by one member, but without this Patrick would not have been able to research the gang. This then leads to the problems associated with staying in the group. Again James Patrick found this too problematic. Living with the violence of the group proved too much for him. The researcher then has to find a way out of the group. It was relatively easy for Festinger and his researchers because the 'end of the world' did not arrive and the group dissolved. However, for Rosenhan's researchers, getting out of a mental hospital having been diagnosed as schizophrenic could have been more difficult. As it was they were all labelled as schizophrenics 'in remission'.

This is a very useful paragraph which picks up marks for knowledge and understanding and for identification of relevant examples and interpretation of research problems.

A major advantage of observation studies is that the social actors are in their natural setting and, unlike being in a laboratory, they continue with their everyday lives. However, there are disadvantages. If the researcher is overt, there is the problem of the Hawthorne effect as people may change their behaviour if they know they are being observed. Eileen Barker was able to overcome this in part as she spent such a long time with the Moonies that they became used to her. They even used her as a confidante. There are disadvantages here too. It is possible that the researcher loses objectivity and 'goes native' — James Patrick was in danger of this, as he mentioned that he thought of some of the gang members as friends. A further problem lies with representativeness. It is often the case that the group is atypical, so generalisations cannot be made. Terry Williams' study consisted of only eight young men — this is in contrast with Townsend's study on poverty which involved over a thousand people.

This is a very good paragraph describing disadvantages and illustrating the points with appropriate examples.

Ethical issues are relevant too. Disguise and deception may be inevitable in covert research. Whether this justifies the study is always a matter of debate. Laud Humphreys' study not only created ethical problems in that he assumed the role of 'watch queen', but he took registration numbers and surreptitiously entered the names of these men into his health survey. This is not simply unethical, it is illegal.

The material on ethical issues is good, but the essay needs a conclusion, however brief it might be.   AO1: 16/20; AO2: 14/20 = 30/40 marks

This candidate has produced some extremely good responses and demonstrates all the relevant skills.   **Overall: 50/60**

■ ■ ■

Answer to question 3: grade-C candidate

(1) (a) Variables are measured and controlled by researchers in laboratory experiments. The independent variable can be manipulated to bring changes in other variables. An example would be watching a violent scene and becoming aggressive.

The candidate has correctly identified the term and provides an appropriate example.   2/2 marks

(b) If a study is reliable it means that if it is done again by others they will get the same results. Validity means that the data are close to the truth.

 Although this is a brief response, the candidate has identified differences between the two concepts.   4/4 marks

(c) Positivists believe that sociology is a science. Durkheim in his study of suicide used official statistics on suicide because he wanted sociology to be seen as a science. Durkheim took the statistics at face value and didn't look at the meaning of suicide. Positivists use quantitative data because they think it is objective. They look for social laws.

 This student has correctly identified three characteristics of positivism (sociology as a science, social laws and the use of quantitative data), but the question asks for a brief description of three major characteristics. The material on Durkheim is poorly focused on the question and does not score any marks.   3/6 marks

(d) Bandura et al. did an experiment on children and violence on television. He asked children to watch a film of adults hitting a Bobo doll and then they were left in a room with a mallet and a Bobo doll. The children used the mallet repeatedly to hit the doll. The researchers said that the experiment showed that children are affected by violence on TV and simply copy what they watch. However, many people have criticised this method because the children were not in their everyday situation and acted differently in the lab. One child said, 'That's the doll we have to hit, Mummy.'

 The candidate has unnecessarily described the study and spent little time focusing on two problems with the laboratory method. However, the artificiality of the laboratory is identified and in the last sentence the issue of demand characteristics is implicitly addressed. Marks scored = 2 + 0 and 2 + 0.   4/8 marks

(3) Postmodernism is the newest sociological theory and seems to be critical of all the others. Postmodernists call the old theories, such as Marxism, functionalism and feminism, metanarratives or 'big stories'. They argue that these metanarratives are no longer sufficient to help us explain a changing world.

 The candidate is correct in identifying Marxism and feminism as metanarratives, which are criticised by postmodernists.

Postmodernists are very critical of Marxists because they just see two social classes as characterising capitalist societies, whereas postmodernists say that class is not as important as it was. Today people's identities are less related to class or to their work but, as the postmodernists argue, the media are more important for giving people different ideas about identity. Our identities can be created out of a pick-and-mix set of possibilities. Postmodernism is useful in looking at the way high and popular cultures can be seen as moving together. For example, a very famous opera aria, 'Nessun Dorma', was on *Top of the Pops* because it introduced a football championship and people started to buy it in large numbers. Postmodernists like Strinati say that we cannot distinguish between high culture and popular culture when this happens. Postmodernism is also relevant in looking at art and architecture, but is perhaps not so useful if we want to explain Third World poverty or the position of women in some fundamentalist societies.

📝 The candidate makes fair points about class and identity, but this should have been developed further. There is reasonable knowledge and understanding of the popular culture debate, although Strinati analyses postmodernism and would not claim postmodernism as his own perspective. There is relevant evaluation and use of examples here.

An interesting aspect of their argument is that postmodernists see the world as 'fractured and fragmented' — this means that nothing is certain any more. Class and gender aren't fixed. People can pick and mix. People like Judith Butler even talk about gender identity as fluid.

A problem with postmodernism is that if postmodernists challenge all the other theories, does it mean that they have a theory to replace them and does this become a metanarrative too?

📝 Overall, this is a fair response and the candidate has made some relevant points. How could you build on this essay to improve it?

AO1: 11/20; AO2: 10/20 = 21/40 marks

Overall: 34/60

uestion

Secondary research; interpretivism; choice of methods; science and sociology

Section A

Item A

If sociologists wish to use documents in sociological research, whether they are historical or life documents, they must be aware of potential problems. As John Scott (1990) has argued, the test of such documents involves several factors. The documents may not be representative of all relevant documents, they might well be simply the longest surviving. Their authenticity may be untested; it is possible for even supposedly 'great works of art' to be fakes. Finally, their credibility needs to be examined. The author may simply have been driven by the desire to deceive. This last point may be especially true of personal diaries.

Item B

Interpretivists argue that the only way to make sense of social behaviour is to understand the meanings of social action as understood by the individuals who are actually involved in the action. This calls for a considerably different kind of methodology from that used by positivism. Individuals must be studied within their own social contexts and the methods used must be able to get as close as possible to the social reality of those individuals. This demands a great deal of sensitivity on the part of the researcher, and methods such as participant observation are necessarily highly individual techniques.

(1) (a) Explain what is meant by 'life documents' (Item A). (2 marks)

(b) Identify **TWO** advantages of using historical documents in sociological research. (4 marks)

(c) With reference to Item B, give **THREE** criticisms that positivists would make of the interpretivist approach to research. (6 marks)

(d) Examine some of the reasons why participant observation 'demands a great deal of sensitivity on the part of the researcher' (Item B). (8 marks)

Section B

Answer ONE question from this section.

(2) Assess the relative importance of the different factors influencing the sociologist's choice of research method. (40 marks)

(3) 'Laboratory experiments on social behaviour only demonstrate how people behave in laboratory situations.' Assess this statement with reference to sociological arguments and evidence concerning the experimental method. (40 marks)

■ ■ ■

Task

This question is for you to try yourself. Before you begin, it would be useful for you to revise the appropriate sections and look through your notes. You could try to answer the question under timed conditions in $1\frac{1}{2}$ hours. Below are some guidelines to help you with your answers.

Section A

(1) (a) Make sure you read the item carefully and that you do not confuse life documents with historical documents.

(b) The question asks you to identify two advantages of life documents. Make sure that you do all that is required in the question.

(c) Think carefully about this. You are being asked to criticise the interpretivist approach from a scientific position.

(d) The key word here is 'sensitivity'. This will involve you addressing issues of trust, betrayal, confidentiality, deception and the feelings of the group. It would be useful if you were to make reference to these issues in relation to some research examples.

Section B

You now have a choice of essays, but try answering both questions.

For essay **(2)** you will need to weigh up the relative importance of practical, ethical and theoretical factors. One useful way to remember this is PET.

For essay **(3)** you will need to identify appropriate studies that have used the laboratory method and evaluate the interpretivist critique concerning the artificiality of these situations.

A2
Coursework Task

The guidance and advice contained in the following pages are intended for students who have opted in Unit 5 to be assessed by carrying out a piece of coursework rather than sit the written examination.

The A2 coursework task gives you the opportunity to devise, carry out and analyse a piece of sociological research, based on either primary or secondary data. There are obvious advantages of choosing this option. It enables you to focus on an area of interest to you, and to put a particular research method into practice. You will experience at first hand the kinds of issues and problems faced by practising sociologists. This will not only benefit your coursework but also enable you to make pertinent and insightful comments on methodological issues when answering questions on other topic areas, particularly your chosen synoptic topic.

However, the coursework option is far from being an 'easy ride'. It needs careful planning, and usually takes longer than students first imagine. Most students will experience some setbacks and, while these can be positive in that they can enable the development of problem-solving skills and also provide good material for the Evaluation section, it can be disheartening when things do not go according to plan. Remember that you will almost certainly experience some problems, and make sure that you have allowed sufficient time to deal with these.

The most important advice is probably not to be too ambitious in what you set out to do. The mark scheme is focused on the process of planning and conducting research, rather than the actual findings, so take care right from the start not to be over-ambitious in either your hypothesis/aim or in the quantity of data you collect or use as the basis for analysis.

Equally important is the need to keep within the recommended maximum length of 3,500 words. This can be difficult, particularly if the research has generated a lot of data (often the result of using more than one method). However, remember that in a written examination you have a given length of time in which to present your knowledge and arguments. Look on the coursework as imposing the same kind of discipline, except that you are restrained by a word length rather than a time length. It is certainly possible to convey all that you need to in the recommended word length, and straying too far beyond this will not only show a lack of discipline on your part but also take up valuable time from your study of other units or other subjects.

Preparing for the coursework task

If you have chosen the coursework option for the assessment of Theory and Methods, it is important that you approach the task in a systematic way, allowing yourself plenty of time. The first thing, then, is to find out from your teacher not only the final date by which your coursework will need to be submitted for marking, but all the 'internal' deadlines that you will have to meet. Another important task before you start is to familiarise yourself with the mark scheme. You will note that there are two schemes, depending on whether your research is based on primary or secondary data. Read the top band descriptors particularly carefully, as these provide you with the goals you need to strive for to get really good marks.

Coursework diary

From the moment that you start thinking about your coursework, you should start a diary, preferably in a notebook rather than on separate sheets of paper. Mark the notebook clearly with your name, class and school or home address. That way, if you mislay it or leave it on the bus, there is a good chance that it will be returned to you. You should choose the format that best suits you, but the diary should contain notes on all the tasks you do along the way to completing your coursework, including discussions with your teacher, people or organisations you contact (including details of names, addresses, fax and telephone numbers), and the dates that you do these things. Also included should be problems that arise and how you attempt to deal with them and, most importantly, details of all the resources that you use — books, newspapers and magazines, and internet sites. Such a diary will make it much easier for you to write your evaluation and will be invaluable for the bibliography.

Choosing the topic

The best coursework arises from something in which the student has an interest. You will inevitably have found some aspects of some topics more interesting than others, and you should try to build on this. Remember that the 'core themes' can also provide a useful basis for coursework topics. You may wish to develop the coursework proposal you submitted at AS (see below for guidance on this), but many candidates will wish to choose a new subject. However, don't just think of a 'topic' — think of how you would research such a topic and what difficulties you might experience.

You should think of at least two possibilities and make rough notes on each, sketching out a potential aim or hypothesis, and thinking of the context sources and relevant concepts, as well as the method you could use. You should then briefly note any possible problems you might experience in the research, and think of how, and whether, you could resolve them. You should be prepared to reject any possible topic that seems to pose too many problems.

When you are satisfied that you have a reasonable topic (in terms of the aim or hypothesis, context sources, concepts and method), make an appointment to discuss it with your teacher. Going through these steps will ensure you avoid embarking on something that either has to be abandoned or presents you with too many difficulties.

Developing A2 coursework from an AS proposal

Some of you will have already carried out the AS coursework task, and have achieved good marks in this. You may therefore understandably be tempted to take your AS proposal and actually carry out the research for your A2 coursework. However, don't simply assume that everything that you suggested at AS can just be implemented at A2, so that no further planning on your part is required. You need to go through the kind of process described above, and look at your proposal with a critical eye. Planning research that you will not have to carry out in practice is obviously quite a different task from actually having to go through the whole research process. Use the material below to look critically at each section of your AS work. At best, it is likely that you will have to make some amendments, possibly major ones, and at worst, you may have to abandon it and start with something else.

Writing your coursework task

Word length

It is most important that your coursework falls within the maximum recommended word length of 3,500 words. AQA now issues some guidelines for each of the coursework sections at A2. These are only guidelines — there is no requirement for you to keep each section to the suggested word length (though you will have to keep within the maximum of 3,500 words). However, the guidelines will at least give you an idea of the balance between different sections. The guidelines are as follows:

Rationale	150	words
Context	750	words
Methodology	750	words
Evidence	1,150	words
Evaluation	700	words
Total	**3,500**	**words**

Rationale

This is the part of your account where you explain your reason for choosing the topic. You will need to be quite brief, so make every word count. 'I have always been interested in this topic' is not sufficient. You should try to make a sociological point, for example: 'Studying "media representations" made me aware of the many ways, often quite subtle, that the mass media portray and reinforce stereotypes of certain groups in society, and made me wonder about the extent to which such representations influence how audiences think about and behave towards these groups.'

You will also state your hypothesis or aim in this section. This is probably the single most important aspect of your coursework, and something that you must get right. The examiner will see how whatever you have chosen as your hypothesis/aim can be 'tracked' through the rest of your coursework. In other words, everything else that you write about must be related to your stated hypothesis/aim. It is a good idea, as you plan and write your different sections, to keep asking yourself in what way the things you are doing are connected to your hypothesis/aim.

One of the problems for many students is that their hypothesis/aim is just too ambitious. This will often be the case with students who are trying to carry out the research presented in their AS proposal. Remember that the examiner is interested in how you actually plan, carry out and analyse research — the focus is on the process rather than the product. You need to be able to display all the relevant sociological skills, and it is much easier to be successful at this if your initial hypothesis/aim is a manageable one. This is likely to mean in practice that you are researching only a tiny aspect of something, but this doesn't matter — in fact, it will usually be a huge advantage. One of the things that examiners are looking for is whether you did what you said that you were going to do. Choosing a manageable hypothesis/aim makes it much more likely that you will succeed in this respect, irrespective of your actual findings. Be sure to check the suitability of your hypothesis/aim with your teacher before you start your research.

It is often useful to identify two or three objectives (more than this is likely to become unmanageable) which will form the basic structure of your research. Again, if your hypothesis/aim is limited in scope, you will find it easier to identify appropriate objectives and how you intend to attain these objectives. An example might be:

Objectives	Procedure
(1) To draw an appropriate sample to test my hypothesis.	Consider what sampling frames are available and accessible. Choose the most appropriate, decide on the sample size and draw the sample.
(2) To administer a question-naire to the selected group.	Decide what information you need. Write a suitable questionnaire and carry out a pilot study before using it on the sample group.
(3) To analyse the results and draw appropriate conclusions.	Separate out the quantitative and qualitative replies and analyse each. Decide whether the findings support or refute your hypothesis, and why.

Context

In this section you should choose two or three suitable sources (remember the impor-tant link to your hypothesis/aim) which provide 'background' to your research. It is likely to take some time to select the most appropriate context pieces, as you will need to be able to show the way in which they are linked to your hypothesis or aim. For example, one type of source might be a study that forms the basis of your hypothesis — you want to carry out research to test a hypothesis that emerges from the findings of the study. Another type of source might be an explanation or discussion of a partic-ular sociological perspective, such as 'liberal feminist', which has helped you to develop a particular aim. You might also see a report of a new social policy, such as a way of attempting to reduce crime, and decide to explore the reactions of people in the community, or police officers, to the policy. You should provide a brief outline of your chosen context pieces (always remembering that important link to your hypothesis or aim), making it clear how each informs your chosen area of research.

In this section you should also outline some important concepts that you are going to use in your research — in the research design, in carrying out the research and in the analysis of the results. Again, check that the concepts are relevant to your stated hypothesis or aim. You should then make a note in your diary if any of your chosen concepts is likely to be difficult to operationalise, as this is an issue that you will need to address during your research.

Methodology

How you approach this section will partly depend on whether your research will be based mainly primary or secondary sources.

You should make every effort to select and use only *one* method. This is for two main reasons. The first is that using one method will make it easier for you to keep to the maximum word length. The second reason is a point that was made earlier — the examiners are more interested in how you deal with the research *process* than in the actual findings of your research. You will be able to demonstrate all the necessary knowledge and skills, and achieve the highest mark, by using just one method. If you genuinely think that the research would be improved by the use of an additional method, then you can say so, and say why, in your 'Evaluation' section.

If your research is going to generate primary data, then in this section you will have to give an account of the method you have chosen, including your reasons for that choice. Note that you should not simply present a textbook list of the advantages and disadvantages of whatever method you have chosen — remember again the all-important link to your hypothesis or aim. In practice, this means that your discussion of the reasons why you have chosen that method will need to be couched in terms of what it is that you are actually researching. For example, a student might say: 'As my aim is to explore the reasons behind some people's decisions to belong or not to belong to a religious group or organisation, a semi-structured interview would allow me both to collect some factual background information for comparative purposes, and also to probe in greater depth people's attitudes to religion and religious teaching.'

Having chosen what you consider the most appropriate method for your research, your next task should be to keep it manageable. Many students get themselves into difficulties by being overambitious regarding what they can achieve in the time and with the resources at their disposal. Remembering again the importance of 'process, not product', be sure to set yourself realistic targets in this regard.

It is difficult to generalise with regard to 'how many', but 10–15 questionnaires will usually be sufficient if you are using the survey method. Interviews generally take much longer than questionnaires to analyse, so if you are conducting unstructured interviews, you will probably not be able to manage more than two. If you are using structured interviews, particularly if these contain a high proportion of closed questions, then you might be able to manage five or six.

Content analysis can also be very time consuming, particularly in the stage of constructing a suitable coding schedule, so don't attempt to use it on too many sources. It is far better to construct a good coding schedule and apply it to just a few newspapers, magazines or programmes than to try to cover a huge number and range of publications or several hours of viewing. Observation based on the 'tally chart' method raises similar issues, so don't be tempted to try to observe more than a few classes or situations.

Remember that the examiners will always be checking to see whether you did what you said that you were going to do. If your targets are realistic and achievable, then you will be able to succeed in what you set out to do.

In this section you should also note the possible problems of using your chosen method *to investigate your initial hypothesis or aim*. This means couching your discussion of potential problems in terms of what it is that you are actually going to research, rather than a list of 'disadvantages' or 'problems' associated with the method in general.

If you are basing your research on secondary data, your account of the methodology chosen will relate to the method(s) used by the author(s) of the data you have chosen. You will have to discuss the reasons for that choice. Some of these are likely to be given in the source material, but you may be able to supplement these with your knowledge of the author(s) and any particular perspective they are associated with, such as Marxism or feminism. This also applies to any associated problems. Some of these will have been mentioned by the author(s), and some you may uncover from a careful reading of the account of the research process and the findings. You will therefore need to choose your secondary source very carefully, to ensure that there is sufficient information there to enable you to write this section.

Evidence

This section is for the presentation of your findings. It is likely to be the longest section of your research, so it needs particular attention. Some students get carried away here, and liberally sprinkle their pages with graphs, charts, tables, pie charts and various diagrams. Many who do this seem to think that simply presenting the information in this way is sufficient. Sadly, they are wrong. You should never leave the evidence to 'speak for itself'. What the examiner is interested in is your sociological interpretation of the information you have obtained. This means that you should think carefully about every 'finding' you include, however it is presented on the page, and analyse it to explain its significance, particularly in terms of your stated hypothesis or aim. In other words, each piece of information you provide from your research should support and illustrate the conclusions you are drawing from it. In terms of your overall schedule, this clearly means that you should leave yourself sufficient time to go through this process of examination, analysis and presentation of findings.

Evaluation

This is where your critical faculties should be at their sharpest. You will need in this section to cast a clear and critical eye over the methodology used (yours if your research is based on primary data; that of the author(s) if you have used secondary data). You should identify what went well, and why, and what gave rise to problems, and why. You should also give a critical evaluation of your findings, and the conclusion(s) you drew from them, again clearly in terms of your stated hypothesis or aim. Remember that your findings must support the statements you make here — the examiners should be able to go back to your 'Evidence' section and see how and why you are able to make the statements that you do. Your evaluation should be both positive and negative, which means that you should be able to state what was good, or went smoothly, as well as discussing the problems and the reasons for them. Remember that if you really think that the use of an additional method would have added to the research, this is the appropriate place to discuss this — with, of course, your reasons. However, there is absolutely no need to do this — your chosen method is quite likely to have been sufficient, particularly if you set yourself a tightly focused hypothesis or aim.

In this section, you should also put forward some recommendations for further research. Again, any recommendations you make should arise logically from your findings (or those of the author(s) of your secondary data). You should give brief reasons why you think that further research along the lines you propose would be beneficial.

Bibliography

This is where you list all the sources used in your research. If you have kept your research diary, this will be a straightforward task. If you are quoting published material, remember to include, as appropriate, the full title, the author(s), the publisher and the date of publication. If you have used a journal of some kind, quote the volume and issue number as well as the date. Newspapers and magazines should be identified by their full title and issue date, and you should give details of the author(s) of the relevant article(s) used. Any websites you have used should also have the address given in full. Remember only to quote in your bibliography those sources you have actually used — sources you looked at and then discarded without taking anything from them (this includes ideas as well as actual material) need not be listed.